FITZGERALD

F. SCOTT

RUTH PRIGOZY

THE OVERLOOK PRESS

WOODSTOCK & NEW YORK

First published in paperback in the United States in 2004 by
The Overlook Press, Peter Mayer Publishers, Inc.
Woodstock & New York

WOODSTOCK:
One Overlook Drive
Woodstock, NY 12498
www.overlookpress.com
[For individual orders, bulk and special sales, contact our Woodstock office]

NEW YORK:
141 Wooster Street
New York, NY 10012

Published by arrangement with Penguin Books Ltd.

Library of Congress Cataloging-in-Publication Data

Prigozy, Ruth.
  F. Scott Fitzgerald / Ruth Prigozy.
    p. cm.
  Includes bibliographical references.
  1. Fitzgerald, F. Scott (Francis Scott), 1896-1940. 2. Novelists, American—
20th century—Biography. I. Title
PS3511.I9 Z827 2001   813'.52—b21 2002283250

Printed in Singapore
9 8 7 6 5 4 3 2 1
ISBN 1-58567-519-9

For Sue, Ted, Maddie and the memory of Stanley Brodwin

CONTENTS

F. SCOTT FITZGERALD

ACKNOWLEDGEMENTS

I should like to thank, first, Caroline Pretty and Pernilla Pearce at Penguin UK, for their advice and help. Others who generously contributed photographs and assistance in obtaining them include Tom Adams, Mary Corliss, John Donnelly, Terry Geeskin, Eleanor Lanahan, Linda P. Miller, AnnaLee Pauls, Frances Ring, Don Skemer, Betsy Schulberg and Charles Scribner III. I should also like to thank Hofstra University for a research leave which enabled me to finish this work.

FITZGERALD

I. PROLOGUE:
THE AFTERLIFE OF F. SCOTT FITZGERALD

F. Scott Fitzgerald died on 21 December 1940, but that date also marks the beginning of his new life as one of the pre-eminent American writers of the twentieth century. It would take another decade for his name to become recognized by scholars and critics, and still another for the general public to become familiar with some version of his life and work. By the end of the century, F. Scott Fitzgerald had perhaps the largest public recognition of any writer in the world: not only does *The Great Gatsby* (1925) boast yearly sales of over 300,000 in the United States alone, but Fitzgerald's name and image also are today firmly engraved on the collective imagination of our culture, both in America and abroad. Scarcely a day passes that we do not note a reference in newspapers and magazines, as well as television and films, to Scott, to Zelda and, above all, to Gatsby; the word 'Gatsbyesque' has entered our vocabulary, identifying one's capacity for romantic wonder, for the power to transmute ordinary experience into transcendent possibility. In a recent listing of the greatest English-language novels of the twentieth century *The Great Gatsby* was ranked in second place by the editorial board of New York publisher Random House's Modern Library, following James Joyce's *Ulysses*. Among critics and scholars, Fitzgerald is regarded as one of the three major American writers of the last century, alongside William Faulkner and Ernest Hemingway.

To achieve an accurate portrait of Fitzgerald, we must distinguish between myth and reality; a difficult task compounded by the author's propensity to create a public personality that quickly became part of the celebrity myth-making so characteristic of public figures in the early decades of the twentieth century. That the dramatic events in Fitzgerald's life readily lent themselves to such myth-making further enhances the difficulty of this task.

We live in an era that celebrates the culture of celebrity, and both Fitzgerald and his wife, Zelda Sayre, possessed the physical attractiveness, charm and effervescence that would endear them to a new decade of public exploitation (the 1920s) as well as engender a virtual orgy of moralistic recrimination from the same public, which found in the couple's personal tragedy a forum for post-Depression, post-World War II discussions of waste, degeneration and even spiritual inertia. We can now recognize that Fitzgerald's life coincided with the rise of new technology that created public personalities who, once in the public arena, often lost control of their carefully cultivated images. The Fitzgeralds became such victims of their own skill at manipulating mass media, as did movie stars such as Clara Bow and 'Fatty' Arbuckle, both victims of the machinery of Hollywood success and public morality.

Today, Fitzgerald and his wife are again celebrated by a public that regards them not only as icons of a fascinating era, but also as models for an age of affluence when fun, good looks, charm and, above all, fame and self-destruction are subjects for endless magazine pieces, television mini-series and undergraduate adulation and emulation. For a true history of F. Scott Fitzgerald, we must pierce the contemporary layer of public renown, return first to the year of his death, and then start from the beginning in

F. Scott Fitzgerald with Zelda, 1923

1896. Only then may we truly comprehend the man, the artist and, indeed, the heroic survivor that was F. Scott Fitzgerald.

II. Prologue: 21 December 1940

When F. Scott Fitzgerald died of a heart attack in the apartment of his lover, Sheilah Graham, he was only forty-four years old, and had seen the flame of his success twenty years earlier extinguished by his wife's mental illness, his use of alcohol, his need for money and the public's changing taste in fiction. But Fitzgerald never failed as a writer: at the time of his death he was writing a new novel, *The Last Tycoon*, which, even in its unfinished state, showed that his brilliance had been undimmed by time and adversity. But in the last year of his life, Fitzgerald had earned less than fifteen dollars in royalty payments and, although six of his works were still in print, he was a forgotten man. Indeed, when young Budd Schulberg was assigned the task of collaborating with Fitzgerald on a screenplay in 1939, he was surprised, thinking the older writer was long since deceased. Newspapers noting his death viewed him as a relic of the 'Jazz Age', and few were willing to concede to him more than, in the words of *The New York Times* (24 December 1940), 'a real talent which never fully bloomed'. The New York *World-Telegram*'s assessment (24 December 1940) is representative of the majority of the obituary commentary on F. Scott Fitzgerald's place in American letters: 'As an interpreter of his times – at least one facet of his times – he was a skillful artist ... But when the gin-

and-flapper era faded he seemed unable to adapt himself ... ' and at his death was 'the sad young man of an almost forgotten interlude in the history of American manners and morals'. Like Herman Melville and other great writers of the past, Fitzgerald was at the end an obscure writer – but his deserved resurrection and ongoing life in the collective imagination of the modern world is a story unique both in its tragedy and triumph. Fitzgerald himself never totally conceded defeat, even when both present and future seemed at their bleakest. At a particularly low point in 1940, he wrote to his editor, Maxwell Perkins, that though he was no longer read, he believed even then that there was little published 'that doesn't slightly bear my stamp – in a *small* way I was an original' (*Letters*, p. 288). His story is, finally, that of a man who was, as he described himself, first and foremost a writer: a man who, through writing, achieved immortality.

THE EARLY YEARS:
ST PAUL AND THE YOUNG WRITER

F. Scott Fitzgerald was born at 481 Laurel Avenue in St Paul, Minnesota, at 3.30 p.m. on 24 September 1896. He was the third child born to Edward and Mary McQuillan Fitzgerald, but the first two children had died in infancy. Fitzgerald weighed ten pounds, six ounces at birth but, despite his size, he was often afflicted with colds and fevers as a child, undoubtedly contributing to his mother's anxiety about her only son. Fitzgerald reports in his *Ledger* that his first spoken word was 'up', which may reflect his goal throughout his life.

Fitzgerald's birthplace: 481 Laurel Avenue, St Paul, Minnesota

Fitzgerald as a baby

Edward Fitzgerald's family had left Montgomery County, Maryland, shortly after the Civil War to settle in St Paul; the

The landmark centre and
statue in St Paul

author is buried in the family plot in St Mary's Church in Rockville, Maryland, birthplace of his paternal grandmother. Her family was descended from the Scotts and the Keys, which made Fitzgerald a very distant (and proud) relative of the composer of the American national anthem. Indeed, he was named Francis Scott Key Fitzgerald. On his mother's side, his ancestors were Irish immigrants who became wealthy in the wholesale-grocery business after the Civil War and lived in the wealthy Summit Avenue section of St Paul. Mary McQuillan, who married Edward Fitzgerald in 1890, was an eccentric woman who, after losing still another child after her son's birth, tended to coddle and overprotect Scott. Edward Fitzgerald was a good-looking, quiet and gentlemanly figure who tried to instil standards of behaviour in his son derived from his own

Fitzgerald's paternal grandmother

Fitzgerald's maternal grandfather

Southern heritage. He filled the young boy's head with legends of the family's history and tales of the Civil War, which made a lasting impression on his son.

Edward Fitzgerald's wicker-furniture business failed in 1898, and the family moved to Buffalo, New York, where he was employed as a salesman for Proctor & Gamble. Edward felt this failure for the rest of his life. In 1926 Fitzgerald thanked his agent, Harold Ober, for a courtesy to his father, remarking, 'His own life after a rather brilliant start in the seventies has been a "failure" – he's lived always in mother's shadow and he takes an immense vicarious pleasure in any success of mine' (*Letters*, p. 393). Both during and after his lifetime, there have been suggestions that Edward was a heavy drinker. Mary, or Mollie, as his mother was called, who was

Top Mollie McQuillan before marriage
Bottom Fitzgerald with his father

not a good-looking woman, was twenty-nine when she and Edward married. Fitzgerald once described her as 'neurotic, half-insane with pathological nervous worry' (*Letters*, p. 199), but it was the McQuillans who provided the Fitzgerald family with financial support throughout the author's early life.

As a child, Fitzgerald was small and handsome, with blond hair, blue-green eyes, and a burning desire to be popular, which remained with him past adolescence. As a young boy, he was sent to private Catholic schools where he was always immersed in the students' social life. Baptized a Catholic, Fitzgerald in his early years was observant, attending mass with his mother and even, at her prodding, reciting from his own writing for the convent. Although he announced that 1917 was his last year as a Catholic (*Ledger*), his early contact with the Church never

Fitzgerald as a child

Fitzgerald, 1899

Fitzgerald, 1906

really left him, and it is not difficult to find evidence of that influence in his works – notably in the short story 'Absolution' (1924).
His St Paul friends (the non-sectarian private school in which he
was enrolled in 1908), however, were not Catholics, and this dif-
ference heightened a lifelong sense he had of always being the
outsider. Indeed, years later, he would remember:

I am half black Irish and half old American stock with the usual exaggerated
ancestral pretensions. The black Irish half of the family had the money and
looked down upon the Maryland side of the family who had, and really had,
that certain series of reticences and obligations that go under the poor old
shattered word 'breeding' (modern form 'inhibitions'). So being born in that
atmosphere of crack, wisecrack and countercrack I developed a two-cylinder
inferiority complex. So if I were elected King of Scotland tomorrow after gradu-
ating from Eton, Magdalene to Guards, with an embryonic history that tied
me to the Plantagenets, I would still be a parvenu. I spent my youth in altern-
ately crawling in front of the kitchen maids and insulting the great. (*Letters*,
p. 503)

By 1908 Edward had lost his job with Proctor & Gamble, and the
family returned from Buffalo. They had spent over a year in
Syracuse, New York, where Scott's sister, Annabel, was born in
1901. In St Paul, Edward worked as a grocery salesman in a real-
estate office owned by the McQuillans, and his young son was
keenly aware of his father's professional and social failure. His
mother placed her hopes in her son as a kind of compensation
for his father's dismal career, although she hoped that he would
achieve success in business, not as a writer. Fitzgerald's embarrassment over his mother's eccentric behaviour and his father's
failure certainly contributed to his sense of being an outsider.

The Fitzgeralds lived for a time with Mollie's mother in the
Summit Avenue section of St Paul and later rented apartments in

the same neighbourhood. The family moved many times, both before and after they settled in St Paul; Fitzgerald himself never owned a home, and continued this early pattern of moving throughout his life. When his first book was published, he described his home, 599 Summit Avenue, as 'In a house below the average/In a street above the average' (*Life in Letters*, p. 33), indicating that the unprepossessing residence still rankled.

Fitzgerald's childhood years in St Paul were important to his development as a writer. Although by no measurement was the family poor, Fitzgerald's friendships with the wealthy St Paul social set made him acutely aware of his family's ambiguous status. He was a member of popular clubs, was even elected a member of the tony White Bear Country Club, but he always felt self-conscious because of his parents' peculiarities and his family's continuing financial dependence on the McQuillans. But because he was a McQuillan, the young Fitzgerald was accepted by the families of St Paul's wealthy residents. Among his best friends were Alida Bigelow, Marie Hersey and Xandra Kalman, with whom the young boy attended dancing classes as well as the local dramatic group, the Elizabethans. All three would remain lifelong friends of Fitzgerald. Although Fitzgerald lived in a pleasant rented row house, the large homes of his wealthy friends were in the adjacent blocks, and the mansion of railroad magnate James J. Hill was a short walk from his home. The young Fitzgerald was thus, like Nick Carraway in *The Great Gatsby*, both a part of their world and, at the same time, an onlooker.

As a young boy in Buffalo, Fitzgerald began to fall in love with girls, and to fight with boys. At the age of nine he was in love with Nancy Gardner, and he recalled vividly his 'love affair' with Kitty Williams in his *Thoughtbook*, a kind of diary that he kept during his early adolescent years. He began it in August 1910 and

Fitzgerald, 1911

kept it until February 1911, thus covering his fourteenth and part of his fifteenth year. Much of the material in the *Thoughtbook* is incorporated in more finished form into his *Ledger: Outline of My Life*, which he began in 1922. The earlier book is a young man's account of his infatuations with girls, his interest in sports and his formation of and association with clubs – 'the white handkerchief', 'the boys' secret service of St Paul', 'the Gooserah Club' and 'The Scandal Detectives'. The latter is the subject of a later Fitzgerald story of the same name. The importance of the *Thoughtbook* is its revelation of F. Scott Fitzgerald as a natural storyteller – using dialogue and dramatization of events – and, equally, how important the opinions of others were to the young boy. Entries in both the *Thoughtbook* and the *Ledger* indicate how fascinated the young Fitzgerald was by acting, appearing whenever possible in dramatic presentations at school, at camp, and later at social clubs. His first play, *The Girl from Lazy J* (1911), was performed by the Elizabethan Dramatic Club, with the author starring in the melodrama written for one actor. Another play, *Captured Shadow*, was performed the next year by the club in a local girls' school, and the following year, 1913, he was cast in his own Civil War drama,

Cast of *The Coward*, 1913

The Coward, shown at the YWCA and later at the White Bear Yacht Club. His last play for the club, in 1914, was *Assorted Spirits*, in which he not only had a major role, but also served as stage manager.

Fitzgerald began writing fiction even earlier: his first published work, 'The Mystery of the Raymond Mortgage', appeared in 1909 in *Now and Then*, the paper published by St Paul Academy. In his *Ledger* entry for that year, Fitzgerald said he wrote that story along with two others. He was thrilled to see his story in print, having waited anxiously for the copies to arrive and shouting, 'They're here, they're here!' on their delivery. Actually, his first recorded entry about his writing was in 1907, where he stated, 'He began a history of the U.S. and also a detective story about a necklace that was hidden in a trapdoor under a carpet. Wrote celebrated essay on George Washington and St. Ignatius' (*Ledger*).

Fitzgerald in high school

Football team at Newman School, 1912.
Fitzgerald is second from the left in the front row

Only 'The Mystery of the Raymond Mortgage' survives (it was later reprinted in *Ellery Queen's Mystery Magazine* in March 1960).

In June 1911 Fitzgerald reports in his *Ledger*, 'No work at school,' which was undoubtedly one of the reasons the family enrolled him in the private Catholic Newman School near Hackensack, New Jersey. Fitzgerald was never a disciplined student, and it is clear that his interests in literature, in theatre, in sports and in social activities would always supersede the requirements of the classroom. That summer he smoked his first cigarette, and noted the popular song 'Alexander's Ragtime Band', composed by Irving Berlin, who would remain his favourite songwriter throughout his life.

Life at Newman School was not easy for the young Fitzgerald. He wanted desperately to succeed – perhaps too much – in all those areas of life that interested him. He said that he felt life's infinite possibilities, and so he threw himself into every endeavour that captured his interest, with the result that he more often than not felt defeated rather than elated. He made the Newman football team but, in trying to avoid the physical assaults that were part of the game, he was accused of cowardice. He soon became the butt of other students and found himself once again the outsider. When he saw Sam White, a noted Princeton pass-catcher in the Harvard–Princeton game, Fitzgerald decided he would go to Princeton.

Fitzgerald found solace for his isolation at school in the New York theatre, particularly the musicals, which he loved and which inspired him to compose his own librettos. He saw Ina Claire in *The Quaker Girl* and Gertrude Bryan in *Little Boy Blue*. Years later he would remember his first glimpses of New York City, which so enchanted him that he captured them vividly in 'My Lost City' and *The Great Gatsby*. In the former, he recalls that 'New York City had all the iridescence of the beginning of the world' (*Crack-Up*, p. 25), and in *The Great Gatsby*, Nick Carraway's appreciation of the city is Fitzgerald's which began when he was a teenager: 'The city seen from the Queensboro Bridge is always the city seen for the first time, in its first wild promise of all the mystery and the beauty of the world' (p. 55). When he discovered the Princeton Triangle Club, which put on a musical show each year, he was more than ever determined to go to Princeton.

He did make one friend at Newman, Sap Donohue, another mid-Westerner, popular at school, and appreciative of Fitzgerald's talents. In the spring term, his grades improved and he was successful in the junior field meet. But, typically, he so basked in his success that he bragged and became overbearing – and again was relegated to the sidelines. An unfortunate incident on the football field (avoiding an open tackle) made him again the butt of his classmates' scorn, and his sense of personal failure was profound. Those years of struggle, intermittent triumph and crushing defeat were indelibly captured more than fifteen years later in the Basil Duke Lee stories that were published in *The Saturday Evening Post*.

Perhaps the most important event of his Newman years was meeting Father Sigourney Fay, later Monsignor Fay, a school trustee and later its headmaster. Father Fay was round, funny and sophisticated, and he and the young Fitzgerald became immediate friends (replicated in the friendship of Amory Blaine and Father Darcy in *This Side of Paradise*, 1920). Father Fay had a personal income, which allowed him to live well, and he was a lover of poetry (which he also wrote). He introduced the young student to Shane Leslie, like Father Fay a convert to Catholicism, and a noted writer, sophisticate, and a first cousin of Winston Churchill. Some years later, Fitzgerald would remember Shane Leslie as 'the most romantic figure I had ever known. He had sat at the feet of Tolstoy, he had gone swimming with Rupert Brooke, he had been a young Englishman of the governing classes when being one must have been, as Compton MacKenzie says, like being a Roman citizen' (*In His Own Time*, p. 134). After sparkling conversations with the two men, Fitzgerald very briefly entertained the idea of becoming a priest, but their influence on him was not primarily religious. Rather, through them, he saw another level to which he might aspire – and the fact that the two men were Catholics became central to his idea of himself as part of a world of brilliance and sophistication.

Fitzgerald continued writing at Newman and published three

of his efforts in the *Newman News*. Like the four stories he had written at St Paul Academy, these showed a skill at language, dialogue and the romantic imagination that would characterize his later work. These stories are different, however, in that the first two, 'The Luckless Santa Claus' and 'The Trail of the Duke', introduce young women as 'femmes fatales' (patterned undoubtedly on his early crushes), and he uses New York City as the central setting for both. In anticipa-

Monsignor Fay

tion of his later work, the stories of this period deal with wealth and social stratification.

Fitzgerald's academic record at Newman was not impressive; even in English, his grades were average. He wrote in his *Ledger* that it was, with the exception of his Christmas vacation at home, 'a year of real unhappiness'. He had started drinking at Newman and in the April *Ledger* entry for the year wrote that he was 'tight at Susquehanna'. He took the entrance exams for Princeton and returned home to wait for his acceptance notice, while producing his own play, *The Coward*. Shortly after he returned home, his Grandmother McQuillan died, leaving her daughter sufficient funds to pay for Scott's Princeton tuition. Finally, although his entrance tests were not strong enough to admit him, Princeton relented after a strong interview at the university, and he was admitted, with conditions (which meant passing exams in Latin, algebra, physics and French in December) as a member of the class that would graduate in 1917.

PRINCETON, GINEVRA KING

When Fitzgerald entered Princeton he was filled with enthusiasm. Here, he felt, would be his opportunity to fulfil his dreams of social success, and perhaps to find acclaim in athletics. Once again, early enthusiasm would end in despair, yet the Princeton years served as a source of his first triumph as a writer, the friendships he made there would last throughout his lifetime, his literary interests would deepen, and the thrilling parties and football games would never fade from his memory.

When he entered Princeton, Fitzgerald was five feet eight inches and weighed one hundred and thirty-eight pounds. Although he was small and slight, he tried out for the football team (the famous Hobey Baker, Princeton's greatest player and the model for Allenby in

Fitzgerald with friends in freshman outfits, Princeton, 1913

This Side of Paradise, was captain, and not much taller than Fitzgerald) and was rejected – a blow that he would always remember. Without question, the young Fitzgerald expected too much from Princeton, but it is understandable that a boy from St Paul, educated at a middle-range Catholic school, would look to Princeton as an opportunity to enter a social world he had dreamed of from his childhood. For at Princeton, he was still an outsider, not part of the new group of students from fashionable prep schools like Hotchkiss, Exeter and Andover, and an onlooker at their social milieu.

Princeton in the pre-World War I days was an enclosed world whose traditions had remained unchanged for twenty-five years. It was a small undergraduate college with about 1,500 students and an acceptable library of over 250,000 books. The campus was much smaller than it is today, but the buildings were old and impressive. For the university, football was the most important activity, and the Yale and Harvard games were major events of the year. Clearly, success in football meant social success, and Fitzgerald's disappointment in this field led him to search out other avenues where he might acquire social distinction. He saw the Triangle Club, which produced musical shows, and the *Princeton Tiger*, the humour magazine, as his best means to excel, and soon began writing the musical comedies that would consume his time and energy at Princeton. He also made new, lifelong friends among the students who, no matter which social stratum they were from, were intellectuals, poets and scholars, like Edmund Wilson, John Peale Bishop, Alexander McKaig and John Biggs, Jr. (later to become the executor of Fitzgerald's meagre estate).

Because he was pulled in so many directions other than that in the classroom, Fitzgerald barely passed his first semester.

Although he noted in October 1913 that he was 'Tight in Trenton' (*Ledger*), he was apparently not a habitual drunkard (the fact that he noted when he was drunk would seem to confirm this judgement). He returned to St Paul for Christmas and in January 1914 took an exam for a course he had not finished during the regular semester. His contribution to the Triangle Club, *Fie! Fie! Fi-Fi!,* was selected for production, but he was given credit only for the plot and lyrics (the president of the club had altered his text). In April of that year, he met John Peale Bishop, who was to exert a profound literary influence on Fitzgerald, particularly in poetry. It was through Bishop that he developed his love for Keats, who remained his favourite poet throughout his life. He met Edmund Wilson as well, who years later Fitzgerald would describe as his 'literary conscience'

John Peale Bishop

Edmund Wilson

Ginevra King

(*Crack-Up*, p. 79). By June he had passed all of his courses except coordinate geometry, but his grades were poor. Nevertheless, he was continually reading, and Compton MacKenzie's *Sinister Street* and the works of H. G. Wells were significant influences on his own writing.

In the autumn semester, once again he failed geometry and as a result was not allowed to appear in his own Triangle Club play. The play toured the country, however, and Fitzgerald relished his first taste of celebrity, both at Princeton and in St Paul, where he attended a performance. When he returned home for Christmas vacation, he met a beautiful sixteen-year-old girl, Ginevra King of Lake Forest, Illinois, who was visiting his old friend Marie Hersey. He fell deeply in love with Ginevra, whose social position, beauty and charm he would capture in many short stories and novels, particularly in Isabelle in *This Side of Paradise*, and Judy Jones in 'Winter Dreams' (1922), who 'communicated her excitement to him, lavishly, deeply, with kisses that were not a promise but a fulfillment. They aroused in him not hunger demanding renewal but surfeit that would demand more surfeit ... It did not take him many hours to decide that he had wanted Judy Jones ever since he was a proud, desirous little boy' (*Short Stories*, p. 226). His courtship of Ginevra took the form of constant correspondence, and she came to Princeton with her mother that semester to attend a Broadway show.

His collaboration with Edmund Wilson on the Triangle show *The Evil Eye* resulted in credits for the lyrics, but he was again unable to appear in it, although a picture of him dressed as a woman was printed in a number of newspapers, including *The New York Times*. All of the roles were played by males, so the picture was not remarkable except for his extreme good looks. He was deeply disturbed by his continuing academic failure, but a diagnosis of mild tuberculosis allowed him to say that he left the semester early because of ill health; years later, he would remember the significance of his Princeton disappointments. Describing his leaving Princeton, he wrote:

It transpired … that it had been tuberculosis – a mild case, and after a few months of rest I went back to college. But I had lost certain offices, the chief one was the Presidency of the Triangle Club, a musical comedy idea, and also I dropped back a class. To me college would never be the same. There were to be no badges of pride, no medals, after all. It seemed on one March afternoon that I had lost every single thing I wanted – and that night was the first time that I hunted down the spectre of womanhood that, for a little while, makes everything else seem unimportant. (*Crack-Up*, p. 76)

Fitzgerald's last words indicate sexual discretion, even prudishness, but there is no doubt how he sought solace from his great disappointment.

Ginevra was still uppermost in his mind, but she had to leave her own school, Westover, and she soon became interested in wealthier young men. It was on a visit to Ginevra that Fitzgerald heard the words that he would always remember, that 'rich girls don't marry poor boys'. After Fitzgerald returned for the 1916–17 year, Ginevra came to Princeton for the Yale game, but the relationship was clearly over by January, and in a short story, 'The Debutante',

Fitzgerald on a friend's ranch in Montana, 1915
Opposite Fitzgerald in drag for a Triangle Club show

which he published that month in the *Nassau Literary Magazine*, the title character is patterned on Ginevra King. After failing three out of his six courses, Fitzgerald considered joining the armed services as other young Princeton men were doing. The war was not Fitzgerald's primary interest; he was writing for the *Lit* and brooding over his academic failure. A short story, 'The Spire and the Gargoyle', which he wrote in 1917, expresses his regret over his missed opportunity at Princeton. Like the author, the protagonist neglects his schoolwork, for 'Winter muses, unacademic and cloistered by Forty-second Street and Broadway, had stolen hours from the dreary stretches of February and March.' The tower, or spire, represents all that he had yearned for and had given up in pursuit of pleasure – and the gargoyle is the little instructor who refused to pass him. Too late, he sees that 'There was something terribly pure in the chaste stone, something which led and directed and called. To him, the spire had become an ideal. He had suddenly begun trying to stay in college' (*Apprentice Fiction*, pp. 106–7). Clearly, Fitzgerald used his pain and rejection creatively: the loss of Ginevra and his Princeton failure would inspire some of his most important writing. A poem he wrote at this time, later used in his first novel as prose, conveys the pain of his last days at Princeton even in its first line, 'The last light wanes and drifts across the land' (*Nassau Literary Magazine*, May 1917, p. 95). Just two months before he died, he would express to his daughter his distress over a bureaucratic decision that deprived him of fulfilment at Princeton: 'I went back to junior year with Princeton in my pocket and it took them four months to take it all away from me – stripped of every office and on probation – the phrase was "ineligible for extra-curricular activities". I was in the hospital besides. Don't let it happen to you' (*Letters*, p. 94). In his *Ledger*, he wrote at the top of the page for that year: 'A year of terrible disappointments and the end of all college dreams. Everything bad in it was my own fault.' Fitzgerald's capacity to look at his own failures objectively, to see himself – and his protagonists – from a moral perspective (he once referred to himself as a 'spoiled priest') adds a dimension that would deepen the tragic implications in his work.

America entered the war in April 1917; Fitzgerald enlisted in May for a three-week training programme which gave him credit for his three academic courses, though he was never to graduate from Princeton. Father Fay tried to enlist him on a secret mission for the Catholic Church in Russia, but it was cancelled, so he waited for his army commission at Princeton. He received it in October, outfitted himself at Brooks Brothers, and reported to Fort Leavenworth, Kansas, in November. Never observant or noticeably religious, he described this year in his *Ledger* as his last as a Catholic (Father Fay would die in January of 1919, so this declaration is unrelated to his death), and it would also mark the beginning of the relationship that would forever shape his life.

Fitzgerald in uniform

THIS SIDE OF PARADISE, ZELDA SAYRE, EARLY SUCCESS, GREAT NECK

Fitzgerald began writing in training camp and had completed a 120,000-word novel within three months. 'Every evening,' he said, 'I wrote paragraph after paragraph on a somewhat edited history of me and my imagination' (*Afternoon of an Author*, pp. 84–5). *The Romantic Egotist*, as he called it, was rejected by Scribners, although their letter, undoubtedly written by Maxwell Perkins, who would become his lifelong editor and friend, encouraged him to revise the work. The revised version was again rejected in October, but it

Opposite Maxwell Perkins
Below Montgomery Country Club – where Fitzgerald first met Zelda

Zelda as a child

Opposite Zelda as a ballerina

was ultimately the basis for his first successful novel, *This Side of Paradise*.

In June he was sent to Camp Sheridan, outside Montgomery, Alabama, to prepare for overseas service. The young women in Montgomery were excited by the influx of new officers, and the social life was equally stimulating for the young officers – notably for Scott Fitzgerald. In July he met Zelda Sayre at a dance at the Montgomery Country Club, but did not fall in love with her until 7 September, the date recorded in his *Ledger*. That same month, Ginevra King was married.

Zelda Sayre was an unusual eighteen-year-old young woman – without benefit of make-up, she had a natural beauty, with red-gold hair, fine features and a graceful body. She was an extremely popular belle, and Fitzgerald was attracted not only to her considerable charms, but also to her status as the most popular girl. From her childhood she had been rebellious, often playing jokes and outlandish tricks without regard for consequences. Indeed, what distinguished Zelda from Scott Fitzgerald was that she tended to ignore the consequences of her actions, whereas he, particularly after a drunken escapade, would feel keenly the impropriety and embarrassment of his behaviour, frequently apologizing profusely to anyone whom he might have offended. But

Zelda was the perfect girl for the young Scott: beautiful, independent, brilliant in conversation and correspondence, socially prominent (although not wealthy), and as eager as he was for success – although in her case, the goal was amorphous. Certainly, it required of a young woman of her status that she marry someone who could support her and help her towards the success she craved.

Zelda Sayre came from a respectable Southern Episcopalian background. Her father was an Alabama Supreme Court judge, and her mother, Minnie Machen Sayre, was the daughter of a Kentucky senator. The hint of psychological instability in Zelda's family stemmed from her father's nervous breakdown and the suicide of her maternal grandmother, both events never discussed by the family. (Her brother, Anthony, would commit suicide in 1933.) But they provide clues to the origin of Zelda's later psychological illness. Zelda had three older sisters, but she, as the last of five children, was her mother's pride.

Scott and Zelda's love was exciting and difficult from the start. He courted her and she responded, and there is little doubt that their relationship was consummated before he left Montgomery. However, she refused to commit herself to him, for she was well aware of his financial situation. Her elusiveness made her that much more desirable to him, and he was determined to win her at whatever cost. Later, when he was about to marry her, he expressed his love for Zelda, and despite all of the trials and traumas that would characterize their years together, he could never forget that love, nor could he ever desert her. He said, to a friend who criticized Zelda's careless public behaviour:

No personality as strong as Zelda's could go without getting criticisms and as you say she is not above reproach. I've always known that. Any girl who gets stewed in public, who frankly enjoys and tells shocking stories, who smokes constantly and makes the remark that she has 'kissed thousands of men and intends to kiss thousands more,' cannot be considered beyond reproach even if above it. But Isabelle I fell in love with her courage, her sincerity and her flaming self-respect and it's these things I'd believe in even if the whole world indulged in wild suspicions that she wasn't all that she should be.

But of course the real reason, Isabelle, is that I love her and that's the beginning and end of everything. You're still a catholic but Zelda's the only

Fitzgerald in New York, 1919

God I have left now.
(*Correspondence*, p. 53)

Fitzgerald was completely open and direct in expressing his feelings, but at the same time felt that he had a limited emotional capital, and feared that by spending it liberally he would ultimately experience a loss of vitality (he treats this subject fictionally in a short story, 'Emotional Bankruptcy' (1931)). Those who remembered him as a young man recalled his excitement over parties and new experiences, his whole-hearted support for new writers whom he admired (like Ernest Hemingway, Thomas Boyd and André Chamson). He would, without hesitation, tell a young woman that she was the most beautiful girl he had ever seen and, even in later life, he would express his interest in new people and ideas with the enthusiasm of a young man.

Fitzgerald was sent to Camp Mills on Long Island, but the war ended before he could be shipped overseas (another lifelong regret). He took an apartment in New York City and worked at an advertising agency, trying to rewrite his book and to keep up his relationship with Zelda who, although unofficially engaged to Fitzgerald, was dating other men. On his arrival in New York he had sent her a telegram: 'While I am sure of you[r] love, everything is possible I am in the land of ambition and success.' But

Fitzgerald, 1919

his situation did not improve, and he grew depressed, drank more frequently, and finally decided to return to St Paul to work on his novel. He knew that he had to achieve the success that would allow Zelda to accept his proposal. He had bought her an engagement ring, but she was unwilling to accept him as her prospective husband because of his limited prospects, and they quarrelled frequently.

He worked at 599 Summit Avenue in the summer of 1919 and, in September, sent Scribners his novel, which was accepted within two weeks. Thrilled with his success, he wrote to all of his friends, and felt sufficiently confident to send off nine stories, all of which were accepted by popular magazines. (His first commercial magazine story was published before the novel's acceptance: 'Babes in the Woods' in *Smart Set*, September 1919.) His first *Saturday Evening Post* story, 'Myra Meets His Family', was

Scott and Zelda, 1920

Overleaf This Side of Paradise jacket cover, 1920

41

THIS SIDE OF PARADISE

By F. Scott Fitzgerald

published in March 1920, marking his long association with that magazine. In November, he travelled to Montgomery and his engagement to Zelda was now official. But his days of uncertainty and despair found expression in some of his most memorable stories, 'May Day' (1920), 'Winter Dreams' (1922) and 'The Sensible Thing' (1924). And he would recall over ten years later the sudden shift from desperation and failure to dizzying success in his biographical essays 'Early Success', 'My Lost City' and 'Echoes of the Jazz Age' (*Crack-Up*).

This Side of Paradise was published on 26 March 1920, and Scott and Zelda were married at the rectory in St Patrick's

From the film *Bernice Bobs Her Hair*, with Shelley Duvall and Murray Moston, directed by Joan Micklin Silver, based on Fitzgerald's short story published in *The Saturday Evening Post*, 1920, and collected in *Flappers and Philosophers* the same year (John Springer Associates)

Cathedral on 3 April. They spent their honeymoon at New York hotels, first the Biltmore, which they had to leave because their behaviour disturbed other guests, and then the Commodore, where they continued their exuberant celebration, initially by circling in the revolving doors of the entrance for a full hour.

Fitzgerald described his book as 'a novel about flappers written for philosophers', and it made him an immediate celebrity. It continued to sell out each printing and, by the end of the following year, it had sold almost 50,000 copies (a respectable number, though not nearly as popular as the top ten best-sellers). In the same year, Scribners brought out a collection of Fitzgerald's early stories, *Flappers and Philosophers*, and the first film made from a Fitzgerald short story, *The Chorus Girl's Romance* (based on 'Head and Shoulders'), opened in 1920.

This Side of Paradise is an autobiographical first novel, a coming-of-age story which coincides with the decade that embraced a youth culture as the nation sought its own new identity in the post-World War I years. The changes America was experiencing from 1912 through to 1919 were faithfully captured in the novel, particularly those concerning the relations between the sexes. Fitzgerald captured the mood of the nation, as expressed in dialogue, dramatizations, songs, moral discussions and the swiftly changing manners that his protagonist, Amory Blaine, witnesses and absorbs. Princeton figures prominently in the novel, as Amory becomes embroiled in the social politics of the school. Like Fitzgerald, Amory cares about popularity and, like the author, is ultimately disappointed by his inability to triumph at his undergraduate career. He explores radical politics and social-climbing, and finds sex linked with the problem of evil – or the presence of the Devil. The novel is, finally, a search for maturity, and the ending is uncertain, but open. He has tasted failure at Princeton, has lost the girl he loved, but has also begun to find himself, to search for answers beyond those provided by his own ego. Monsignor Darcy, his mentor, has guided him towards becoming a 'personage' rather than a 'personality', someone who acts and defines himself by his actions, rather than one who succeeds through his charm. At Monsignor Darcy's funeral, Amory realizes that his life must have meaning, and it will if he learns to serve others. '"I know myself," he cried, "but that is all"' – the memorable last line of the novel – reflects the emotional honesty of the whole work. For despite its unevenness, it is a genuine expression of feeling by a young man who seems to speak for his generation.

Zelda in the garden

Zelda with jewelled pin in her hair

Left George Jean Nathan
Right H. L. Mencken

The critics were not unanimous in praising the novel; there were many errors overlooked by copy-editors and Fitzgerald was blamed for its illiteracy; Edmund Wilson did note later, however, that despite its many failings, 'it does not fail to live' (*In His Own Time*, p. 405). But John Peale Bishop wrote to his friend, 'it's damn good, brilliant in places, and sins chiefly through exuberance and lack of development' (*Correspondence*, p. 49). H. L. Mencken in *Smart Set* called it 'the best American novel that I have seen of late' (August 1920), and *The New York Times* praised it too, noting that 'the glorious spirit of abounding youth glows throughout this fascinating tale ... As a picture of the daily existence of what we call loosely 'college men', this book is as nearly perfect as such a work could be ... It could have been written only by an artist who knows how to balance his values, plus a delightful literary style' (*Critical Reputation*, p. 5).

The photographs of the handsome young novelist and his beautiful wife, along with tales of their antics, filled the newspapers and magazines, and the Fitzgeralds did everything possible to live up to their celebrity which coincided with the start of the 'Jazz Age', so aptly named by Fitzgerald himself. Zelda saw herself as the new flapper, and her own interviews and articles reinforced the public's perception of the couple as overgrown children having a riotous good time – diving fully clothed into the fountain at the Plaza Hotel (Fitzgerald noted that he was sober at the time); riding down Broadway in open cars; attending parties that lasted until dawn; drinking and dancing until they collapsed. Their friends included several from Fitzgerald's Princeton days,

and major figures in the literary and theatrical worlds, like George Jean Nathan and H. L. Mencken, co-editors of *Smart Set* magazine, which published his short-story masterpiece 'The Diamond as Big as the Ritz' in 1922 (it had been rejected by the mass circulation magazines).

But it was not only the Fitzgeralds who were experiencing the new age so intensely: he described the Jazz Age as 'a whole race going hedonistic, deciding on pleasure' ('Echoes of the Jazz Age', *Crack-Up*, p. 15). His own success seemed enchanted, bewildering:

I was adopted, not as a Middle Westerner, not even as a detached observer, but as the arch type of what New York wanted ... I, who knew less of New York than any reporter of six months' standing and less of its society than any hall-room boy in a Ritz stag line, was pushed into the position not only of spokesman for the time but of the typical product of that same moment. ('My Lost City', *Crack-Up*, pp. 26–7)

He would never forget his golden moment of early success, 'when the fulfilled future and the wistful past were mingled in a single gorgeous moment – when life was literally a dream' ('Early Success', *Crack-Up*, p. 90).

The Fitzgeralds needed a respite from their frenetic

Opposite left Scott and Zelda ('Rolling Junk'), 1920
Opposite right Zelda in knickerbockers, posing in front of the Marmon, 1920
Right Fitzgerald's agent, Harold Ober

social pace and lavish expenditures, and so they rented a house in Westport, Connecticut, from May through to the September of 1920. The parties continued there, but they still found it dull and moved back to the city for a few months. In July they travelled in a second-hand Marmon touring car, dressed in matching white outfits, to Montgomery. Later, Fitzgerald published a three-part article, 'The Cruise of the Rolling Junk' (1922), accompanied by amusing illustrations of the couple. After learning that Zelda was pregnant, they sailed for Europe in the spring of 1921 to enjoy a brief trip abroad before the baby was born. Fitzgerald sent his agent, Harold Ober, a typed copy of his new novel, *The Beautiful and Damned*, on

Top Fitzgerald writing, early 1920s

Bottom Scott and Zelda (pregnant) in Dellwood, White Bear Lake, Minnesota, September 1921

Scott and Zelda in Montgomery, 1921

Zelda with Scottie

which he had been working for the past year.

In England, Fitzgerald met John Galsworthy, St John Ervine and Lennox Robinson, all noted writers, and looked up his old friend Shane Leslie. But the couple found Europe boring, and particularly disliked Italy. Fitzgerald saw the publication of his first novel in England, where sales were disappointing, as they would

Above Ledger page for 1921

Overleaf From the film *The Beautiful and Damned*, 1922, with Kenneth Harlen and Marie Prevost

be for all of his endeavours. They returned after two months and decided to await the birth of their child in St Paul, where their friend, Xandra Kalman, attended to the details of their settling in and awaiting the baby, a girl, Frances Scott Fitzgerald (Scottie), born on 26 October 1921. Despite the parties and social activities which they enjoyed, both Scott and Zelda were bored in St Paul, and Zelda in particular could not bear the cold weather.

Their financial problems continued despite Scott's success. The sale of *This Side of Paradise* to the movies for $10,000 helped (the film was never made); *The Beautiful and Damned*, published in March 1922, with two additional printings the same year, totalled about 50,000 sales, but the income from the novel did not free him from the need to publish short stories. A movie was made from the novel the same year, but the rights brought him only $2,500.

The Beautiful and Damned is very different from *This Side of Paradise*; although Fitzgerald thought that readers might think it autobiographical (particularly because it is about a couple, Anthony and Gloria Patch, who in many ways resemble the

Scott with Zelda in a squirrel coat. Gloria in *The Beautiful and Damned* 'wanted a grey squirrel coat'

Tales of the Jazz Age jacket cover, 1922

Fitzgerald in the 1920s

Fitzgeralds), the author here is interested in the society that has produced the couple and their friends, the world of business, advertising, religion, movies and other aspects of popular culture. Through a naturalistic account of the lives of the couple, Fitzgerald explores the meaning, or rather, as Anthony reflects on it, 'The Meaninglessness of Life' (p. 47). The reviews of the novel were mixed. Many saw it as a more mature work than the earlier novel, and were impressed with its vitality. Others found it trivial or depressing, and several noted that the characters were not worth the novelist's effort. But H. L. Mencken offered praise that Fitzgerald would cherish, calling the novel an '*adagio* following the *scherzo*' of *This Side of Paradise*, declaring that Fitzgerald 'ceases to be a *Wunderkind* and begins to come into his maturity' (*Critical Reputation*, p. 35).

In September, his second

collection of short stories, *Tales of the Jazz Age*, was released, and sales were larger than those for his earlier collection. But Fitzgerald then,

Room above the garage at No. 6 Gateway Drive, Great Neck, where Fitzgerald wrote short stories and started thinking about Gatsby

From *The Saturday Evening Post*, 'The Popular Girl', 11 and 18 February 1922

Published Weekly

The Curtis Publishing Company

Cyrus H. K. Curtis, President
C. H. Ludington, Vice-President and Treasurer
F. S. Collins, General Business Manager
Walter D. Fuller, Secretary
William Boyd, Advertising Director

Independence Square, Philadelphia

London: 6, Henrietta Street
Covent Garden, W.C.

THE SATURDAY EVENING POST

Founded A°D¹ 1728 *by* Benj. Franklin

Copyright, 1922, by The Curtis Publishing Company in the United States and Great Britain
Title Registered in U. S. Patent Office and in Foreign Countries

George Horace Lorimer
EDITOR

Churchill Williams, F. S. Bigelow,
A. W. Neall, Arthur McKeogh,
T. B. Costain, Associate Editors

Entered as Second-Class Matter, November 16,
1879, at the Post Office at Philadelphia,
Under the Act of March 3, 1879
Additional Entry as Second-Class Matter
at Columbus, Ohio, at Decatur, Illinois, at
Chicago, Illinois, and at Indianapolis, Ind.

Entered as Second-Class Matter at the
Post-Office Department, Ottawa, Canada

Volume 194 | 5c. THE COPY | PHILADELPHIA, PA., FEBRUARY 11, 1922 | $2.00 THE YEAR by Subscription | Number 33

THE POPULAR GIRL

and for the rest of his life, struggled financially to meet his obligations. Although he notes in his *Ledger* that he would go 'on the wagon' to write short stories, he also notes bouts of drinking. Clearly, his social drinking was escalating into alcoholism, but Fitzgerald never drank to the extent that he became financially irresponsible: indeed, it is a tribute to his devotion to his craft that, whenever he needed additional funds, he was able to focus completely on his work and turn out the stories that would alleviate his financial indebtedness to Ober and Perkins. In 1924, when his expenses far exceeded his income, he retired to the room above his garage next to his home at 6 Gateway Drive in Great Neck where, cold sober, he produced in one winter ten stories that would allow him to focus his attention on the new novel he was contemplating (*The Great Gatsby*). His price at this time for a *Saturday Evening Post* story was $1,750; it would rise to $4,000 by 1929. Fitzgerald was a professional writer, and the best testimony to his professionalism is the quality of his output, which remained high until the day he died.

The question of the quality of his short stories was raised by Fitzgerald himself – and later by Hemingway, who felt that his friend was squandering his talents on inferior work. Undoubtedly Fitzgerald wrote many stories that he knew would find a ready market in *The Saturday Evening Post*, but there is no record of his ever revising a story to make it conform to popular taste. Many of the early stories concerned young people, their desire for success, their search for popularity and love – and these stories echoed the author's own search for goals that he had long found both attractive and elusive. Yet he was unsparing in his criticism of the very rich, of a world that was closed to the aspiring 'sad young men' of his fictional world, and if he
was a popular writer for the   *Opposite* Scott and Zelda in 1932

No. 6 Gateway Drive, Great Neck

Below Party at Great Neck house. Fitzgerald is third from the left in the front row

magazines it was because so much of what he said struck a chord in the imagination of his contemporaries. He referred to many of his stories as 'trash', but he didn't really believe that they were. He put enormous effort into the 160 stories he produced, and the writing in even the slightest efforts is often superb. He 'stripped' many stories of passages he felt worthy of inclusion later in his novels, and more than half a dozen of his stories are gen-

erally acknowledged as among the greatest American short stories ever published.

Continuing their nomadic pattern, the Fitzgeralds lived in Great Neck from mid-October 1922 through to April 1924, travelling to and from New York City in a second-hand Rolls-Royce. They would often be found by their house-man asleep on the lawn the morning after a particularly riotous celebration in the city the night before. Great Neck was about twenty miles from New York City, and it was a popular residence for theatrical people, the new rich, and his new friend, writer Ring Lardner, whose own sad decline into alcoholism Fitzgerald witnessed with sympathy and a recognition of his own propensities. With characteristic generosity towards other writers who needed help, he assisted Lardner in collecting stories for a new volume for Scribner's, his own publisher, which ultimately released half a dozen of Lardner's books.

Fitzgerald had been working on a play, *The Vegetable*, a political satire, which after publication had its try-out in Atlantic City. He had hoped that his play would relieve his financial worries, but it was a flop, closing immediately, and so the Fitzgeralds decided to go abroad, where living expenses would be much reduced (they were about $7,000 ahead after the short-story sales), and where he might continue work on the novel about which, when he had first thought about it two years earlier, he had told Maxwell Perkins, 'I want to write something new – something extraordinary and beautiful and simple + intricately patterned' (*Correspondence*, p. 112). His time in Great Neck provided much of the background for *The Great Gatsby*: scenes from West Egg, the lavish parties at the Swope estate and elsewhere on the peninsula, the Becker-Rosenthal case, and Arnold Rothstein and the Black Sox scandal. (In the novel, Wolfshiem

Ring Lardner

alludes to Herman Rosenthal, a minor underworld figure who refused to pay extortion money to a corrupt New York City police-man, Charles Becker. After Rosenthal told his story to the news-papers, he was murdered. Wolfshiem is based on Arnold Rothstein, the gangster who reportedly fixed the 1919 baseball World's Series, an event known as the Black Sox scandal.) Fitzgerald knew that this was to be his great literary work, and he wrote to Perkins before they left for Europe, 'In my new novel, I'm thrown directly on purely creative work – not trashy imagin-ings ... This book will be a consciously artistic achievement & must depend on that as the first books did not' (*Letters*, p. 163). Their life in Great Neck had become so disordered that he thought that a geographical change would give him a new cre-ative start. He wrote in 1924, 'We felt that we had escaped from extravagance and clamor and from all the wild extremes among which we had dwelt for five hectic years ... We were going to the Old World to find a new rhythm for our lives, with a true convic-tion that we had left our old selves behind forever ... ' ('How to Live on Practically Nothing a Year', *Afternoon of an Author*, p. 102). His relationship with Zelda, who was uninterested in housekeeping, was marked by quarrels and reconciliations, as it had been since they had met. But she grew bored when he was writing and sought her own amusements, which worried him. He was jealous of her flirtatiousness, and her extravagance (Perkins wrote that money went through her fingers like water – she want-ed everything), as well as her adventures in pursuit of amuse-ment, distracted and surprised him, although Andrew Turnbull said that they complemented each other in chaos, like 'gin and vermouth in a martini, each making the other more powerful in their war with dullness and convention' and that Fitzgerald was just as extravagant as his wife (Turnbull, *Scott Fitzgerald*, p. 141).

Writer John Dos Passos, who visited the Fitzgeralds in Great Neck and accompanied them on one occasion to an amusement park, noted Zelda's unusual mental state:

The gulf that opened between Zelda and me, sitting up on that rickety Ferris wheel, was something I couldn't explain. It was only looking back at it years later that it occurred to me that, even the first day we knew each other, I had come up against that basic fissure in her mental processes that was to have such tragic consequences. Though she was so very lovely I had come upon something that frightened and repelled me, even physically ... Through it all I felt a great respect for her, a puzzled but affectionate respect. (*The Best Times*, 1966; quoted in Bruccoli, *Some Sort of Epic Grandeur*, p. 175)

John Dos Passos

EUROPE, EDOUARD JOZAN,
THE GREAT GATSBY, ERNEST HEMINGWAY

After a brief stop in Paris in 1924, the Fitzgeralds went to St Raphael on the French Riviera, not yet the fashionable summer mecca it would become years later. They rented a lovely home, the Villa Marie, in Valescure, where Fitzgerald worked on his novel. But in the summer Zelda, left on her own while Scott worked, began a relationship with a French aviator, Edouard Jozan, part of a group the couple were friendly with at the beach. Zelda enjoyed the attention, and Jozan was clearly taken with her; it is unlikely that it was ever more than a romantic infatuation on the part of both, but when Scott found out about it, he was furious over what he regarded as a betrayal. He never took relationships lightly – and did not approve of sexual promiscuity (his own sexual relationships with other women occurred after

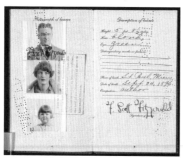

Left Fitzgerald family passport photograph
Opposite, top The Fitzgeralds on a street in Paris, 1924
Opposite, bottom left Fitzgerald family, c. 1924
Opposite, bottom right Fitzgerald with Zelda and Scottie, 1924

The Fitzgeralds

Zelda's breakdown, when the marriage was, in effect, over). Both of the Fitzgeralds embellished the story to their friends, and all that we can be certain of is that neither ever forgot it. She incorporated the Jozan romance into her novel, *Save Me the Waltz,* and Fitzgerald wove it into his portrait of Daisy and Gatsby's lost illusions in the novel he was writing. In his *Ledger* he noted the 'big crisis' on 13 July, but in August he wrote, 'Zelda and I close together.' Yet he remained hurt by the episode: 'That September of 1924, I knew something had happened that could never be repaired' (*Notebooks*, p. 113).

Gerald Murphy
Sara Murphy

Later that summer, they met Gerald and Sara Murphy, an extraordinarily attractive, elegant and cultivated couple who were staying at Cap d'Antibes. Although not enormously wealthy, the Murphys lived well; he was the heir to the Mark Cross stores and Sara came from a well-to-do

background. The Murphys entertained the leading figures in the arts: Picasso, Cole Porter, Fernand Leger, Philip Barry, Dos Passos, Archibald MacLeish, and Fitzgerald's circle of acquaintance grew as his friendship with them deepened. He liked and admired the couple, and aspects of Sara Murphy – notably her

Top left Composer Cole Porter
Top right The Fitzgeralds, Paris, Christmas 1924
Left Archibald MacLeish

elegance – were incorporated into the character of Nicole Diver in *Tender is the Night* (1934), Fitzgerald's novel set on the Riviera.

Before the couple left on a trip to Rome and Capri in the autumn of 1924, Fitzgerald wrote to Maxwell Perkins about a young writer he admired, recommending that Scribners look him up immediately. His name was Ernest Hemingway, whom Fitzgerald would meet – at the Dingo Bar in Montparnasse – in May 1925, when his family was living in Paris after the April publication of *The Great Gatsby*. The trip to Italy was not successful; Fitzgerald never liked

Annabel Fitzgerald's wedding photo, 1925

the Italians, whom he found rude and untrustworthy. On one occasion when he was drunk, he was beaten by the police – a frightening episode that he would later incorporate into *Tender is the Night*.

Reviews of *Gatsby* were mixed; the overriding judgement was that Fitzgerald represented the Jazz Age, and that, at best, *Gatsby* was a novel of limited scope, with disagreeable or immature characters, and a trivial subject. Many praised the author's cleverness, and several concluded that it was a more considerable achievement than his earlier novels. A few major critics praised the novel, but Mencken, while admiring the writing, found it only

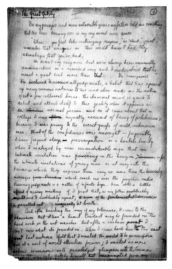

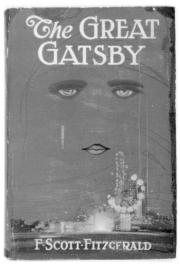

First manuscript page of *The Great Gatsby*

Original jacket of the first edition of *The Great Gatsby*, 1925, painted by Francis Cugat. Maxwell Perkins, Fitzgerald's editor, said that 'it seems a masterpiece for this book'

'a glorified anecdote' (*Critical Reputation*, p. 66). But noted critic Gilbert Seldes praised it without reservation: 'Fitzgerald has more than matured; he has mastered his talents and gone soaring in a beautiful flight, leaving behind him everything dubious and tricky in his earlier work, and leaving even farther behind all the men of his own generation and most of his elders' (*The Dial*, August 1925, p. 162). Fitzgerald was deeply disappointed by the reviews of *Gatsby* but letters of praise from writers he admired assuaged the pain. T. S. Eliot called it 'the first step that American fiction has taken since Henry James' (*Crack-Up*, p. 310) and Willa Cather, Gertrude Stein and Edith Wharton wrote him complimentary letters.

From the 1926 film of *The Great Gatsby*. Gatsby and Daisy
meet at Nick Carraway's for the first time in five years

Gatsby was a departure from the contemporary novel in form
and style, but because it did not use techniques such as stream
of consciousness, which signalled modernist experimentation,
critics could not easily categorize the work, and too often sum-
marily rejected it. It would take years before the world would
recognize the importance of the novel's central concern: a search
for moral order, exemplified in Nick Carraway's quest for the truth
of Gatsby's life, and for the transcendent meaning of human
existence, through Gatsby's unending pursuit of his dream. For
Gatsby's dream at the end is the dream of Everyman, not only for
the young man from the West searching for his lost love, but for
all of us who yearn for more time, perhaps for that 'orgastic
future', and regret wistfully what has been lost. At the end of the

Alan Ladd and Betty Field in the 1949 film of *The Great Gatsby*, directed by Elliot Nugent. Here, Gatsby and Daisy during their earlier courtship

Alan Ladd in the 1949 film of
The Great Gatsby

novel, despite the powerful image of loss, we share Gatsby's romantic hope. Like him, we are beating *against* the current. That final image of the individual pursuing his destiny, however fruitless that pursuit may prove, is the greatness of Gatsby, and perhaps of us all.

In May 1925 Fitzgerald conceded the novel's poor sales at home, and in England, once again, a Fitzgerald novel failed to appeal to the reading public. But neither Fitzgerald nor his contemporaries ever forgot *Gatsby*. He wrote to his wife in 1930 that he had 'dragged *The Great Gatsby* out of the pit of my stomach in a time of misery' (*Correspondence*, p. 239). At the time of his death, fifteen years later, the novel and its writer were extolled by

Robert Redford, Mia Farrow and Sam Waterston as Gatsby, Daisy and Nick in the 1974 film version directed by Jack Clayton

Sam Waterston, Mia Farrow and Robert Redford in the 1974 film of *The Great Gatsby*
Opposite Ernest Hemingway

Glenway Wescott, John O'Hara, Malcolm Cowley and old
Princeton friend John Peale Bishop. Fitzgerald had known the
risks of writing the novel in a new way. He refused to relinquish
his plan, from the outset, to focus on a mood, or 'hauntedness ...
rejecting in advance ... all of the ordinary material for Long
Island, big crooks, adultery theme & always starting from the
small focal point that impressed me – my own meeting with
Arnold Rothstein for instance' (*Letters*, p. 551).

The Fitzgeralds took an apartment in Paris at 14, rue de Tilsitt,
on the Right Bank, and after a month in Antibes where he
enjoyed the Murphys' warm hospitality, Fitzgerald returned to the
city, where he resumed his acquaintance with Hemingway, who
soon became a close friend.

Gertrude Stein

The Hemingway–Fitzgerald friendship has been the subject of much discussion, particularly following the publication of Hemingway's somewhat fictionalized, posthumously published memoir, *A Moveable Feast* (1964). Written at least thirty years after the events described, Hemingway's portrait of Fitzgerald is as much an attempt to deflate his friend's reputation as it is to recount their adventures together. Hemingway's portrait of his former friend, Gertrude Stein, is equally devastating, and lends weight to *Esquire* magazine editor Arnold Gingrich's belief that, had both writers lived longer, Fitzgerald would have remained a friend of his, while Hemingway would have become an enemy.

Fitzgerald always behaved as though he had to bear the major burden of any friendship, had to entertain, fascinate, absorb – in some way affect – others, much as Dick Diver does so effortlessly in *Tender is the Night*. In the early days, their friendship was based on mutual respect. They spent hours together in Paris cafés discussing writers and writing. Fitzgerald generously aided Hemingway with several loans and their letters indicate that their contacts were always pleasant. True, Hemingway always objected to the Fitzgeralds' unannounced incursions, frequently past mid-

night and often bearing unmis-
takable signs of inebriation, into
his domestic life. Fitzgerald
apologized for such episodes,
and once blamed Zelda's
behaviour on 'nervous hysteria'
which had necessitated a morphine injection (*Letters*, p. 295).
Hemingway's complaints, however, were minor annoyances to
Fitzgerald, for in 1926 he wrote
to Hemingway, 'I can't tell you
how much your friendship has
meant to me during this year
and a half – it is the brightest
thing in our trip to Europe for
me.' He continued to offer to
do anything at all for his friend:

Ernest Hemingway with son,
Bumby, Garoupe Beach, 1926

for 'human help under any head – remember you can always call
on your devoted friend, Scott' (*Letters*, p. 298).

But events in the lives of both writers permanently changed
their relationship: Hemingway achieved notable success with *The
Sun Also Rises* (1926), and his own domestic life was marked by
discord, divorce and remarriage. Fitzgerald's life was changing
too: financial pressures intensified, and Zelda began to show
signs of mental illness. Work on his new novel went slowly, and
he notes in his *Ledger* both his drinking and his attempts to go
on the wagon. Hemingway refused to give Fitzgerald his new
Paris address, and repeatedly, and often publicly, disparaged his
friend, especially when Fitzgerald's physical and financial condition had so deteriorated as to render him a defenceless target.

The incident in 1929, when Fitzgerald, serving as timekeeper for a boxing match between Hemingway and Morley Callaghan, accidentally let a round go too long, resulting in Hemingway's knockdown, infuriated Hemingway. The match created still another barrier to their friendship. When *Tender is the Night* appeared in 1934, Hemingway tied in his appraisal of the novel in a letter to Fitzgerald with criticism of the author's personal life. And he wove a scornful description of 'poor Scott Fitzgerald' into his short story 'The Snows of Kilimanjaro'. Deeply hurt, Fitzgerald responded to Hemingway, asking him to 'please lay off me in print', and to Maxwell Perkins, asking that his name be removed from the body of the story (it was later changed to 'Julian'). Although he admitted to Perkins that 'Somehow I love that man no matter what he says or does,' he had already conceded that he was unable, in his present despair, to face the much more successful Hemingway. Hemingway too was unwilling to publicly acknowledge the help Fitzgerald offered – and which he used – in editing *The Sun Also Rises*. In *A Moveable Feast*, Hemingway's attack was centred on Fitzgerald's drinking and on what Hemingway said were Fitzgerald's doubts about his sexual prowess.

Clearly, each writer's response to the other was based on mutual personal need. Fitzgerald was an incurable romantic and needed an embodiment for his dreams of personal heroism and physical superiority, and he found that embodiment in Hemingway. Hemingway always detested public displays of feeling, which he identified with weakness and effeminacy. In his ill-concealed attempt to exorcise doubts about his own virility, in his painful over-assertion of strength, Hemingway seems to have selected Fitzgerald as an alter ego, a repository for his own very real insecurities and sexual worries. Fitzgerald, unconsciously,

seems to have responded to the weight of Hemingway's obses-
sion by becoming outwardly the walking model of Hemingway's
fears, the symbol of his despair. And Hemingway in turn was
goaded by Fitzgerald's abject admiration into virulent displays of
'virile' arrogance and scorn. As the years passed, Hemingway's
fears of sexual and artistic ineffectuality led to those ungenerous
outbursts that culminated in the slyly nasty attack on Fitzgerald
in his memoir. Here, his self-doubt is at the core of a calculated
derogation of Fitzgerald's virility, artistic integrity and human dig-
nity. Indeed, Zelda's accusation that her husband and
Hemingway were having an affair attests to the severity of her
own, not her husband's maladjustment. The friendship between
Fitzgerald and Hemingway is a fascinating study in personality,

Belles Rives Hotel, Juan-les-Pins; formerly Villa St Louis, where Fitzgerald and Charles
MacArthur locked a band in a room so that they might have music

both private and public, and it reveals the way in which a culture steeped in celebrity-worship affects the lives of those who have become part of the mythology of success.

A third volume of short stories, *All the Sad Young Men*, was published in February 1926. This volume was Fitzgerald's most impressive collection, containing such major stories as 'The Rich Boy', 'Winter Dreams', 'Absolution' and 'The Sensible Thing'. It received favourable reviews and sold a respectable 16,170 copies that year, earning him almost $4,000. In March the Fitzgeralds returned to the Riviera, renting villas in Juan-les-Pins. Hemingway needed a place for his family, and the Fitzgeralds moved from their villa, which they allowed the Hemingways to occupy, to the Villa St Louis, where they would remain until the end of the year. It was on the Riviera that Fitzgerald and Hemingway were in close contact, and where Fitzgerald wrote his long letter suggesting cuts in *The Sun Also Rises*. Hemingway's conviction that Zelda Fitzgerald was insane seemed to him to be confirmed by her conversations with him that summer. The two had disliked each other at their first meeting in Paris, and Hemingway was later to say that Zelda had wanted to wreck Scott.

A dramatic version of *The Great Gatsby* had opened on Broadway in February, and the first filmed version was released the same year, bringing Fitzgerald $25,000 less commissions. That summer, he began working on his next novel, but there were many distractions on the Riviera, and his drinking caused tension in his friendship with the Murphys. Indeed, both Scott and Zelda behaved erratically: he clearly because of his drinking, and she because of her increasing mental instability. One night, for example, when the couple were dining with the Murphys at the Columbe d'Or restaurant in St Paul-de-Vence, Zelda, jealous of Scott's interest in speaking to Isadora Duncan, the famous

Playwright Charles MacArthur

dancer, who was at a nearby table, threw herself down a flight of stone steps. The couple seemed to be engaged in a duel – who could be more outrageous? They dived from dangerous heights into the Mediterranean and, both drunk, drove the car erratically along winding roads. Once, they fell asleep in their car on a trolley-trestle and were rescued by a farmer who pulled them to safety the next morning. After a quarrel at a party, Zelda threw herself under the wheels of their car and goaded Scott to drive over her – and he began to do so. But despite such behaviour, Gerald Murphy remained Fitzgerald's lifelong friend. He said:

What we loved about Scott was the region in him where his gift came from, and which was never completely buried. There were moments when he wasn't harassed or trying to shock you, moments when he'd be gentle and quiet, and he'd tell you his real thoughts about people, and lose himself in defining what he felt about them. Those were the moments when you saw the beauty of his mind and nature, and they compelled you to love and value him. (quoted in Tompkins, *Living Well Is the Best Revenge*, pp. 109–10)

Fitzgerald had a drinking companion in playwright Charles MacArthur, and their exploits were notorious, like locking a band in a room in the Villa St Louis to continue playing for them. In his *Ledger*, Fitzgerald wrote, 'Futile, shameful useless ... Self disgust. Health gone.' At the end of the year, the Fitzgeralds returned to America.

HOLLYWOOD, ELLERSLIE, TRAVELS, ZELDA'S BREAKDOWN

After a brief visit to Montgomery, Fitzgerald was invited to Hollywood to try his hand at screenwriting – in particular, a comedy for the popular actress Constance Talmadge. The payment was excellent – $3,500 immediately, and $12,500 if the scripts were accepted. Leaving Scottie with Fitzgerald's parents, who

Scott and Zelda in Hollywood with Wallace Beery, 1927

Carl Van Vechten

Opposite Lois Moran

were now in Washington, DC, Scott and Zelda stayed in Hollywood for two months, where they shared a set of rooms at the Ambassador Hotel with actors Carmel Myers and John Barrymore and writer Carl Van Vechten. Fitzgerald met a beautiful eighteen-year-old film actress, Lois Moran, who had achieved prominence as the daughter in *Stella Dallas* in 1925. He was entranced by her, and admired not only her beauty and talent, but also her commitment to her career. She liked Fitzgerald, and arranged for him to have a screen test, but nothing came of it. She lived with her mother, a widow, and Fitzgerald never had an affair with her. None the less, Zelda became increasingly jealous of his attentions to Lois, and they quarrelled frequently, Scott goading Zelda to fury by extolling Lois's professional career. One night, Zelda burned her clothing in the bathtub at the Ambassador, and their fights about Lois escalated. His script, *Lipstick*, was rejected, but Fitzgerald did meet the young Irving Thalberg, head of production at MGM, who made a lasting impression on him. Both Lois Moran and Thalberg were inspirations for characters in Fitzgerald's work: Lois for Rosemary in *Tender is the Night* and Thalberg for both Miles Calman in his memorable short story 'Crazy Sunday' (1932) and Monroe Stahr in his unfinished final novel, *The Last Tycoon*. Fitzgerald's behaviour

Irving Thalberg, head of production at MGM Studios, and his wife, actress Norma Shearer

in Hollywood, like Zelda's, was erratic: he drank heavily, and once, at a party, tried to make soup out of the guests' jewellery. Zelda, still angry with him over his flirtation with Lois, threw her husband's expensive gift from 1920, a platinum watch, out of the train window as they left California. They had spent more money than he had earned, and they headed back East to look for a place to live where he might be able to work on the novel and new short stories that would pay their debts.

With the help of John Biggs in March 1927 they rented a large home near Wilmington, Delaware, called Ellerslie. After a series of parties, Fitzgerald tried to get down to work. His progress on the new novel was slow and fitful: he had started with the idea of a matricide plot, but eventually shifted to the story of incest and deterioration that would characterize the lives of Nicole and Dick Diver in *Tender is the Night*. Zelda, always interested in becoming a dancer, took ballet lessons and practised constantly. She also wrote several articles for magazines (using both their names as required by the editors). By the summer, Fitzgerald was writing short

The Fitzgeralds en route to France, 1928

93

stories again (several would be used as material for the new novel), many of them of surprisingly high quality considering his excessive drinking. The relationship between the Fitzgeralds was still strained, and they decided to spend the summer of 1928 in Paris so that Zelda might study dancing with Madame Lubov Egorova, a noted teacher. Fitzgerald's short-story fees from *The Saturday Evening Post* had now risen to $3,500, but he had borrowed heavily and, although his income at the end of the year was its highest yet, netting him $30,000, he still needed to publish additional stories to support their life in Paris. He wrote nine stories about Basil Duke Lee, based on his own childhood, and they brought him $31,500.

Zelda worked furiously at her ballet with Mme Egorova,

Sylvia Beach and James Joyce in Shakespeare & Co. bookstore

and Fitzgerald, left to himself,
went drinking, and twice land-

Fitzgerald judging the
Woodbury Soap beauty contest

ed in jail. He met James Joyce in June (he admired Joyce so much
that he offered to jump out of the window to prove it), and later
became friendly with a young French writer, André Chamson,
whom he championed to Scribners and to Hollywood producer
King Vidor. The couple returned to America in October, the novel
still unfinished, Zelda still determined to become a ballet dancer,
and Fitzgerald again turning to short stories. He wrote a haunt-
ing story about a young Southern woman, 'The Last of the Belles'
(1929), which explores the meaning of the South, its women in
particular. He earned extra money by agreeing to serve as a judge
for the Woodbury Soap beauty contest with John Barrymore and
Cornelius Vanderbilt, Jr. A picture of him gazing at one of the
photographs shows again his extraordinary good looks, which
seem undiminished by time and dissipation.

Fitzgerald with Zelda and her mother, Mrs Sayre

In the spring of 1929, when their Ellerslie lease expired, the family went again to Paris, and again the stories he wrote to help pay their way are superior: 'Rough Crossing', 'The Swimmers' and 'Two Wrongs' (all 1929). All three deal with tensions between marriage partners, reflecting the difficulties – 'rows and indifference' – in Fitzgerald's own marriage. His short-story price was now $4,000, the highest he would reach. Again, this trip to Paris resulted in a drunken brawl, and although Fitzgerald reported to Perkins that he was making progress on his novel, he had actually done very little work on it. In his *Ledger* for 1929 he wrote: 'Thirty-two years old (and sore as hell about it) OMINOUS No Real Progress in ANY way & *wrecked myself with dozens of people.*' They travelled to North Africa in February, and after a summer in Cannes returned to Paris in October. Fitzgerald was concerned about Zelda's intense ballet practice. Friends suspected that she was close to a breakdown. On 29 October, the Wall Street stock market crashed (Fitzgerald had not invested in stocks, so that did not directly affect him) and on 23 April of the following year, Zelda was admitted to the Malmaison Clinic outside Paris for nervous exhaustion. Fitzgerald wrote in his *Ledger*, '*The Crash! Zelda and America!*'

Zelda's condition worsened and she was admitted first to Valmont Clinic in Switzerland and then to Prangins Clinic outside Geneva. The two began a series of letters to one another, both trying to account for the terrible collapse of their marriage and their dreams:

You were going crazy and calling it genius – I was going to ruin and calling it anything that came to hand ... and I think everyone far enough away to see us outside of our glib presentation of ourselves guessed at your almost megalomaniacal selfishness and my insane indulgence in drink ... We ruined ourselves – I have never honestly thought that we ruined each other. (*Correspondence*, p. 241)

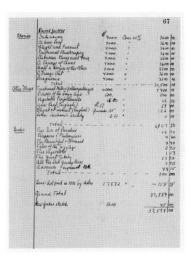

Ledger page for 1931

In their anger, each tried to assess the faults of the other, but throughout this sad display of their recriminations, the letters also reveal their closeness and their mutual love. When Zelda found out that Mme Egorova did not see a future for her as a ballet star, Fitzgerald worked on polishing her writing efforts at Prangins for publication, hoping that it would build her confidence.

During Zelda's stay at Prangins, Fitzgerald was under considerable pressure to write stories to pay for her care, which totalled $13,000. He sold seventeen stories between 1930 and 1931, earning over $37,000, which would be his largest income until he later settled in Hollywood. Much of Fitzgerald's sadness and sense of loss went into one of his greatest stories of this period, 'Babylon Revisited' (1931), about Charlie Wales, who lost his wife and custody of his child in the crash, both he and his wife victims of the excesses of the boom. Fitzgerald captured in a 1931 essay, more poignantly than any other writer, the sense of loss accompanying the end of that wild and exciting era:

Now once more the belt is tight and we summon the proper expression of horror as we look back at our wasted youth. Sometimes, though, there is a ghostly rumble among the drums, an asthmatic whisper in the trombones that swings me back into the early twenties when we drank wood alcohol and every day in every way grew better and better, and there was a first abortive shortening of the skirts, and girls all looked alike in sweater dresses, and people you didn't want to know said 'Yes, we have no bananas,' and it seemed only a question of a few years before the older people would step

Opposite Fitzgerald in France, *c.* 1937
Above Thomas Wolfe

99

aside and let the world be run by those who saw things as they were – and it all seems rosy and romantic to us who were young then, because we will never feel quite so intensely about our surroundings any more. ('Echoes of the Jazz Age', *Crack-Up*, p. 22)

On a trip to Paris in 1930, Fitzgerald met Thomas Wolfe, the six-foot-six writer whose first novel, *Look Homeward, Angel*, Perkins had edited for Scribners. Wolfe was suspicious of Fitzgerald, who genuinely admired his work. Wolfe would later incorporate Fitzgerald as the character Hunt Conroy in his novel *You Can't Go Home Again* (1940).

In the autumn of 1930, Fitzgerald lived in Lausanne, visited resorts in the area, and began having affairs with other women, possibly as a reaction to Zelda's attacks on his masculinity. She said he failed to satisfy her sexually, and while these remarks may testify to the effect alcohol had on him, it is equally plausible that she was reacting to her own strong feelings for Mme Egorova,

which, as she recounted in a letter to her husband from the clinic, she felt were abnormal. Scottie was in Paris with her governess, although she did come to spend vacation time with her father, and to visit her mother. Fitzgerald's devotion to his daughter was expressed by his extreme concern over every aspect of her life – and it would remain constant until his death, when she was in

Zelda 'recovered', 1931

college. When his father died in 1931, he attended the funeral in Washington, DC. As Zelda's condition improved, they took brief trips together to Montreux and Geneva, and in July of that year the family vacationed in Annecy. By the summer Zelda was allowed to live outside Prangins, and by September she was officially discharged. The Fitzgeralds left for the United States that month, having lived abroad for four and a half years.

RELAPSES, LA PAIX, *TENDER IS THE NIGHT*

After returning to Montgomery, Fitzgerald was invited by Metro-Goldwyn-Mayer Studios in Hollywood to work on a screenplay, *Red-Headed Woman*, for actress Jean Harlow, for which he was paid $1,200 a week for six weeks. Irving Thalberg wanted Fitzgerald but, again, it was an unsuccessful venture and his screenplay was not used. He did, however, attend a party at the Thalbergs' (Norma Shearer, the noted actress, was Thalberg's wife), where he embarrassed himself by performing a comic song while drunk. He used that episode in 'Crazy Sunday', one of his finest stories, which was rejected by the major magazines but published by Mencken's *American Mercury*.

Zelda's condition was clearly deteriorating and, after a trip to Florida, he took her to the Henry Phipps Psychiatric Clinic of Johns Hopkins University Hospital in Baltimore. He returned to Montgomery to be with Scottie. While at Phipps, Zelda worked on a novel, which she sent to Maxwell Perkins without informing her husband. The novel, *Save Me the Waltz*, drew on the same experiences Fitzgerald was using in his own novel. He felt betrayed because her novel had been written while he was working on short stories to pay for her care, forcing him to neglect his work on *Tender is the Night*. After a number of accusatory letters, she agreed to alter her novel according to his wishes, and he helped with the editing. Scribners accepted the novel for publication in the autumn of 1932.

In May they moved into La Paix, a Victorian house on the estate of the Bayard Turnbull family outside Baltimore. Zelda, discharged from Phipps, worked on her painting, notably a series of ballet dancers, and continued to practise her own dancing. Fitzgerald produced fewer stories than he had in the past; it was clear that he was no longer able to write the kind of stories about young love and aspiring young men that *The Saturday Evening Post* had looked upon so favourably in the past, and he could find no new subjects acceptable to the magazine. He later wrote to a magazine editor:

It isn't particularly likely that I'll write a great many more stories about young love. I was tagged with that by my first writings up to 1925. Since then I have written stories about young love. They have been done with increasing difficulty and increasing insincerity ... I know that is what's expected of me, but in that direction the well is pretty dry and I think I am much wiser in not trying to strain for it but rather to open up a new well, a new vein. You see, I not only announced the birth of my young illusions in *This Side of Paradise* but pretty much the death of them in some of my last *Post* stories. (*Letters*, p. 588)

His last story brought in only $2,500 and he reported his earnings in 1932 as under $16,000. His health was suffering also, and he was treated at Johns Hopkins for typhoid fever and mild inactive tuberculosis. For the next four years, he would return to the hospital twice a year for treatment of alcoholism as well as his other ailments.

While at Phipps in 1932 Zelda had written a play, *Scandalabra*, which was produced by a local Baltimore company in the spring of 1933. Fitzgerald helped her to edit it, and tried to become an advocate for the production, but it was poorly reviewed and closed. *Save Me the Waltz* was published in October 1932, in a printing of 3,010 copies of which fewer than half were sold. The reviews were poor, and it would take years for critics to appreciate her elaborate metaphorical style. Although she was evidently brilliant, her talent was that of the gifted amateur. She had little skill in novelistic structure, and her writing lacked the discipline of a professional writer. The novel was clearly autobiographical, an attempt to deal with her childhood, the severe tensions in her marriage – plus an extra-marital relationship – and, above all, her breakdown.

Andrew Turnbull, who was only eleven years old when the Fitzgeralds moved to his family's estate, recalled the author as looking both old and young for his years. He remembered his

courteous informality, the faint smile on his trenchant, mobile face, and his eyes that were neither hard nor green ... but gray-blue, faraway, and full of the pathos of burned-out desires. His conversation was taut with emotion and he seemed always to be analyzing or appraising as he talked ... Under the impact of this charming, unpredictable man with his gift for intimacy, life on our place began to vibrate to a faster, subtler rhythm than we had ever known (*Scott Fitzgerald*, p. 211)

The Turnbull children regarded him as a magician, and they saw how he adored his daughter, the two becoming particularly close during Zelda's increasing periods of instability.

Despite having to write stories to support the family, he continued working on his novel. In June 1933 misfortune struck when a fire broke out in an upstairs fireplace where Zelda had tried to burn something. The damage was limited to one area, and Fitzgerald asked the Turnbulls to postpone the repairs until his novel was completed. He worked steadily, although he relied on gin to keep him going. He told Perkins in October 1933 that he had a complete draft, and he and Perkins discussed revisions until it was ready for serialization in *Scribner's* magazine.

Zelda was re-admitted to Phipps in the February of 1934, and then briefly to Craig House in Beacon, New York. To buoy her spirits, Fitzgerald arranged a showing of her paintings at a gallery in New York City but, like her earlier attempt at playwriting, it was unsuccessful. By May her condition had worsened, and she was admitted to Sheppard-Pratt Hospital near Baltimore in a catatonic state. Fitzgerald now knew that she would never recover and, indeed, their marriage had come to a virtual end. He and Zelda would never live as husband and wife again. He wrote

Below Painting, *Times Square*, by Zelda Fitzgerald

Opposite Self-portrait of Zelda Fitzgerald   in his *Notebooks*, 'I left my
capacity for hoping on the little
roads that led to Zelda's sanitarium' (p. 204). He would always
treasure the memories of their early years, and, because of her
illness, he would never divorce her. Their letters during the last
six years of his life are elegiac, filled with memories of their love,
their wild adventures, their limitless expectations, and their
inexorable defeat.

Tender is the Night was published on 12 April 1934, and the first
printing (7,600 copies) sold out, as did two more, totalling an
additional 8,000 copies. The novel reached the middle of the best-
seller lists for two months, but earned its author only about
$5,000, which did not relieve his debts. It is remarkable that, with
the tragic conditions of Zelda's confinement, his own ill health and
alcohol dependency, he was able to continue writing stories and
short essays. The reviews of the novel were mixed: because of the
passage of so many years since the publication of *Gatsby*, expectations ran high for the new work. But most critics felt that there
were structural weaknesses in the novel: Rosemary Hoyt's point of
view in the opening is not sustained throughout the novel. The
chronology seemed confusing to some, and many agreed that
there was insufficient cause for Dick Diver's deterioration. But,
once again, critics whom Fitzgerald respected recognized the brilliance of his work. As he had with *Gatsby*, Gilbert Seldes praised
the novel unreservedly; Fitzgerald, he wrote, 'has stepped again to
his natural place at the head of the American writers of our time'
(*New York Evening Journal*, 12 April 1934, *Critical Reputation*, p. 86).
Burton Rascoe, in *Esquire*, called it Fitzgerald's 'maturest' novel,
his 'rich, Celtic, romantic imagination' having been 'subjected to
the discipline of reflection and selection' (*Critical Reputation*, p.
86). Robert Benchley, an old friend, called it 'a beautiful piece of

Profile of Fitzgerald, used as model for cover of *Tender is the Night*, 1934

work', and said that he hadn't had a book take hold of him in that way for years (*Correspondence*, p. 358). Zelda praised the book too as a 'tragic and poetic personal drama against the background of the times we matured in' (*Correspondence*, p. 353). Fitzgerald later revised the novel to make the chronology clearer, but the response when it was published after his death was mixed, many feeling that the earlier version was superior.

Tender is the Night is the story of Dick Diver, a young psychiatrist, who is seduced by the loveliness of the wealthy young Nicole Warren, whom he has been hired to treat. Eventually they marry, and Dick becomes part of the Warren establishment, used and ultimately discarded by Nicole after she has been cured and the Warren family no longer needs his services. But the bare outline of the story cannot describe the power of the novel: a picture of expatriate Americans and the wealth that ultimately corrupts; an examination of America and its history; and a poignant tale of loss, particularly moving in its reflection of the Fitzgeralds' own lives. The novel achieves a genuinely tragic dimension as it traces the decline of Dick Diver, which affectingly mirrors Fitzgerald's sense of his own eroded hopes.

Publicity photo for *Tender is the Night*

As he had after publication of his earlier novels, Fitzgerald then worked on a collection of short stories, his fourth, published as *Taps at Reveille* in March 1935. The printing was only 5,100 copies, but the reviews were excellent, and the collection itself contains some of Fitzgerald's finest work, including the Basil Duke Lee and Josephine Perry stories, as well as 'Babylon Revisited'. His indebtedness was not eased by the publication, however, and he was forced to look for new outlets for his stories, as acceptance by the mass magazines was no longer assured.

Opposite Film of *Tender is the Night*, with Jennifer Jones and Jason Robards, Jr, 1962

DEBT, DESPAIR, *THE CRACK-UP*

Esquire magazine became Fitzgerald's steadiest outlet during the last six years of his life; in fact, Arnold Gingrich, its editor, accepted his work without reservation. The problem was the fee: *Esquire* paid only $250 per piece, which, no matter how much he wrote, could not meet the high cost of Zelda's care, Scottie's schooling, and his own maintenance. He borrowed heavily, from Perkins and his mother, and secured advances from Scribners. He had less control over his drinking, and Zelda's several suicide attempts at Sheppard-Pratt intensified his despair. He wrote a moving poem about the loss of his love, his romantic dreams, and the sense of possibility – all tied in with grief over Zelda. After tracing petty arguments from their past, the poem concludes:

> And, though the end was desolate and unkind:
>> To turn the calendar at June and find December
> On the next leaf; still, stupid-got with grief, I find
>> These are the only quarrels that I can remember.
>
>> (*New Yorker*, 23 March 1935)

One of his first pieces for *Esquire*, 'Sleeping and Waking', is a meditation on insomnia, from which he had suffered since the years when he had to stay awake at night to write short stories. It became, however, a prelude to the confessional essays he was to

Portrait of Fitzgerald by David Silvette, oil on canvas, 1935

publish later, as he recounts the 'Waste and horror – what I might have been and done that is lost, spent, gone, unrecapturable.' His dreams now, after the 'catharsis of the dark hours are of young and lovely people doing young, lovely things … ' He ends with a verse that he later expanded; it is infinitely sad in its evocation of lost youth:

> In the fall of '16 in the cool of the afternoon
> I met Caroline under a white moon
> There was an orchestra – Bingo-Bango
> Playing for us to dance the tango
> And the people all clapped as we arose
> For her sweet face and my new clothes —

'Life was like that,' he concludes, 'my spirit soars in the moment of its oblivion ... ' (*Crack-Up*, p. 68).

He took a summer trip with Scottie to North Carolina in 1935, where he lived at the Grove Park Inn while she attended camp (and he had an affair with Beatrice Dance, a wealthy, and married, hotel guest from Texas). His tuberculosis had returned and he was treated by a local doctor, but he continued drinking. He could no longer write the short stories that had once commanded high fees from mass magazines; the years from 1930 to 1936 were a time of trial and error, of struggle for a new style and new fictional forms that could accommodate the emotions, the needs and the ideas of a mature man and his tragic life. Despite the tumult and chaos of his personal life, he managed to publish forty-two stories during these six years, only a half-dozen of which were of decidedly inferior quality.

He returned to Baltimore with Scottie at the end of the summer, but travelled once again to North Carolina in the autumn, leaving her with Baltimore friends. Here, in an inexpensive room in the Skyland Hotel, he wrote the three essays that *Esquire* would publish as *The Crack-Up*: the title essay, 'Pasting It Together' and 'Handle with Care' (February, March and April 1936). The essays

Fitzgerald, 1936

revealed Fitzgerald's struggle with his own emotional state, his inability to care about the things that had once mattered to him, his failure at personal and professional endeavours. They did not, however, address his drinking problem and perhaps, as some have suggested, even attempted to camouflage his alcoholism. His friends responded negatively to the essays, Hemingway in particular, who referred to them as Fitzgerald's 'whining in public'. On the other hand, the essays called attention again to Fitzgerald as a writer, and many who had forgotten him were surprised to find him still functioning creatively.

Zelda's condition deteriorated further at Sheppard-Pratt, and she was transferred to Highland Hospital in Ashland, North Carolina, where Fitzgerald believed their treatment methods would help her. The cost of her care there was $240 a month, but his mother's death in early September that year provided funds that enabled him to pay his debts and to enrol Scottie in the costly Ethel Walker School in Connecticut. Perhaps Fitzgerald's lowest point came in September 1936, when the *New York Post* sent a columnist, Michel Mok, to interview him at the Grove Park Inn. Fitzgerald was not well, and he had been drinking. Mok, quickly taking in the situation,

Fitzgerald's mother
Opposite Fitzgerald photographed by Carl Van Vechten, 4 June 1937

exploited it for a sensational story, headlined, '*The Other Side of Paradise*: SCOTT FITZGERALD, 40, ENGULFED IN DESPAIR', with the subtitle 'Broken in Health, He Spends Birthday Regretting That He Has Lost Faith in His Star.' Mok described him as 'writhing in a hell of despondency ... jittery ... his restless pacing, his trembling hands, his twitching face with its pitiful expression of a cruelly beaten child' (26 September 1936).

Distraught over the article, Fitzgerald reported that he swallowed and then regurgitated an overdose of morphine. His expenses were high, but his income was very low and he borrowed constantly from Harold Ober, who was providing a surrogate family for Scottie. He knew that he needed to make the kind of money that only Hollywood could provide and urged Ober to help him find a place there. His reputation, however, both from his own confessional essays and from the Mok piece, made him less likely to inspire confidence in Hollywood producers. He travelled to New York City in the spring of 1937 to attend a rally in Carnegie Hall, where Hemingway spoke against the fascism spreading in Europe. Scott's friend, Carl Van Vechten, photographed him in front of the Algonquin Hotel, looking pensive, worn and tentative, but still undeniably handsome. Despite his recent adverse publicity, with the help of friends he obtained an offer to work for MGM for six months at $1,000 per week, increasing to $1,250 if his option was renewed. When he left for California, he reported that his debts amounted to over $40,000. He set up a rigid financial schedule where he would receive $400 per week for expenses, the rest to be used to pay off his debts, support Scottie in school and meet the costs of Zelda's treatment. Until his death, despite ill health and the defeat of his dreams, he would scrupulously support his family and attempt to meet his financial obligations.

HOLLYWOOD, SHEILAH GRAHAM, *THE LAST TYCOON*

Fitzgerald's characteristic optimism revived when he returned to Hollywood in July 1937. He had stopped drinking, his financial situation looked promising, and several of his old friends, like Dorothy Parker and Robert Benchley, were there to welcome him. He moved into the Garden of Allah Hotel and satisfied his craving for sweets with over a dozen bottles of Coca-Cola each day. He still suffered from insomnia and used medication both to fall asleep and to awaken in the morning. He had always loved the movies, and he began to study film technique seriously. But he was a changed man. He now tended to avoid groups of writers at the MGM commissary; noted director Billy Wilder remembers seeing him sitting quietly at a table by himself, looking pale and somewhat withdrawn. According to Wilder, the young writers like himself remembered Fitzgerald as an icon from another era, respected him, but would not intrude on his privacy. Only occasionally could his friends persuade him to join them at lunch with other writers. He worked on *A Yank at Oxford* for a week, but it would be difficult to find evidence of his work in that script.

But that summer he met the person who would help him find a fragile stability in his last years: a beautiful young gossip columnist, Sheilah Graham, whose resemblance to the young Zelda Fitzgerald startled him when he first saw her. Born Lily Sheil in a

Sheilah Graham

Fitzgerald with Sheilah Graham in LA

London slum, she had risen to her current position by marrying an older man who had played the Pygmalion to her Eliza Doolittle, and later appearing on the London stage. After her divorce, she tried her hand at journalism, and was hired as a syndicated columnist for the North American Newspaper Alliance. Never as powerful as Hedda Hopper and Luella Parsons, she nevertheless supported herself with five columns a week distributed in a respectable number of newspapers. Ironically, she had never read Fitzgerald's books, and was attracted instead to his charm, his good looks, his enthusiasm, his brilliance, and his interest in her. In fact, she broke off her engagement to the Marquess of Donegall for F. Scott Fitzgerald, with whom she fell deeply in love, and whom she was to help and sustain – albeit with interruptions when he began to drink (she had not known

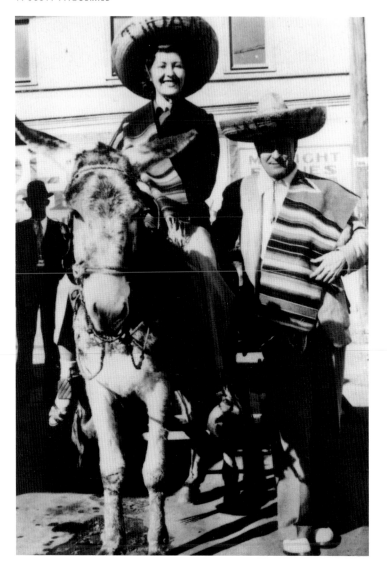

Gregory Peck and Deborah Kerr as Fitzgerald and Sheilah Graham
in the 1959 film *Beloved Infidel*, based on Graham's 1958 memoir
Opposite Fitzgerald with Sheilah Graham in Mexico

he was an alcoholic) and became abusive to her – until his death.
After one serious fight with Sheilah, during which he ridiculed her
background, struck her and brandished a gun, he stopped drinking for a period; and during the last months of his life he
remained sober. Because Sheilah felt keenly her lack of education,
Fitzgerald designed a 'college of one', where he drew up reading
lists of books and music to guide her education. Sheilah bene-
fited from his gift of an education for the rest of her life.

Scottie made several trips to California during Fitzgerald's
years with Sheilah, and he tried to persuade Scottie to pursue
serious matters in school and later in college. Through Sheilah,
she was able to meet her screen idol, Fred Astaire. Zelda, still at
Highland Hospital, never indicated she knew about Sheilah, and

Film, *Three Comrades*, 1938, directed by Frank Borzage, for which Fitzgerald got his one and only screenwriting credit. *Left to right*: Franchot Tone, Margaret Sullavan, Robert Taylor and Robert Young are the principal actors.

Fitzgerald continued to write her concerned, loving letters to which she responded with equal tenderness. The tone of these letters is again elegiac, filled with the memories of their powerful love and poignant realization of its loss.

Fitzgerald's one screen credit, *Three Comrades* (1938), was heavily revised by producer Joseph Mankiewicz, and Fitzgerald was forced to work with another screenwriter, Ted Paramore. He had little respect for Paramore and resented the idea of their being equal collaborators. Yet even the result of that collaboration was altered by Mankiewicz, leaving Fitzgerald exasperated and disillusioned, feelings he conveyed in an emotional letter to the producer. Mankiewicz later said that he had thought Fitzgerald's dialogue was stilted, and that the star, Margaret Sullavan, had objected to some of her lines. Nevertheless, the film was a success at the box-office and was listed as one of the year's ten best. Margaret Sullavan was singled out with an Academy Award nomination as Best Actress of the Year, and she received that honour from both the New York Film Critics Award and the British National Award. Despite Fitzgerald's misgivings about the film and his role as writer, its success resulted in the renewal of his contract at $1,250 per week.

He worked on a number of film projects the next year, but none of them worked out for him. He had a disastrous vacation in the East with Zelda and Scottie, and in April of 1938 moved to Malibu, where Sheilah believed that the tranquillity would help to restore his spirits and encourage his work. At this time, when his daughter was about to enter Vassar, he wrote her a moving letter about his marriage to her mother, telling her that it had been a mistake. Some biographers have felt that he was expressing here genuine regret over his marriage to Zelda, but, in context, this was a letter written primarily as an attempt to save his daughter

Producer Joseph L. Mankiewicz

from the sort of unfulfilled life that he felt would surely result from not having a specific goal. There are also several letters from this period that express his undying devotion to his wife.

Again, Fitzgerald was able to stop drinking for a while, and he worked on a number of screenplays, including *The Women* and, for the last few weeks of his contract, on *Gone With the Wind*. His contract was not renewed, though, and he looked for work as a free-lance screenwriter. He was now living at Belly Acres, a guest-

Edward Everett Horton, actor; Fitzgerald's landlord at Belly Acres

house on the estate of movie actor/comedian Edward Everett Horton. He was hired by producer Walter Wanger to work with the young Budd Schulberg on a screenplay celebrating Dartmouth College's winter carnival. The two were to travel to Hanover, New Hampshire, to immerse themselves in the location, but Fitzgerald and Schulberg began to drink as soon as the plane left California, and the trip was an alcoholic disaster for him. Wanger fired him, and he had to recuperate in a New York

Budd Schulberg when he knew Fitzgerald

Richard Carlson and Ann Sheridan
in the film *Winter Carnival*, 1939

Robert De Niro as Monroe Stahr in the film
The Last Tycoon, directed by Elia Kazan, 1976

hospital, where Sheilah, who had come East on the same plane, attended him. Schulberg finished *Winter Carnival* on his own in New Hampshire.

In 1939, after several fruitless efforts to write his lucrative stories of old, he began to plan a new novel based on his Hollywood experiences; he was to call it *The Last Tycoon*, and it would be based on the recently deceased Irving Thalberg, on his own relationship with Sheilah, and on the changes he had observed in the business of the film industry. And, somehow, the Hollywood story of Monroe Stahr would express, through its depiction of that industry, the changes taking place in the nation and, indeed, in American history. The novel was only half-way finished at his death, but it is a remarkable work, the writing as sharp and eloquent as anything he had ever written; his perceptions and insights into the industry, into the makers and movers in the film world, are mercilessly accurate.

As he had done in the past, he turned again to *Esquire* for the income needed to support his new endeavour. He published the first of seventeen stories about Pat Hobby, a seedy, run-down screenwriter, in January 1940, and *Esquire* continued to publish them monthly even after his death. He and Zelda saw each other for the last time in April 1939, when Fitzgerald took her to Cuba (having had a severe quarrel with Sheilah). The trip ended disastrously when, drinking heavily, he tried to stop a cockfight and was beaten up. It was not until January 1940 that Sheilah reported that she no longer saw him drink – but, by that time, his health had been severely impaired.

Frances Kroll worked as Fitzgerald's secretary during the last twenty months of his life. He was then living near Sheilah, at 1403 North Laurel Avenue in Hollywood, just one block from her apartment. Frances remembers him working on his novel – how

Frances Kroll Ring, 1939

he would leave handwritten pages on yellow lined paper for her
to transcribe, how he would make corrections and she would
retype them, and she recalls how disciplined he was, working in
his pyjamas, robe and slippers until later in the day when he
would dress and dine with Sheilah. He wrote to Zelda, 'I am deep
in the novel, living in it, and it makes me happy. It is a *constructed*
novel like *Gatsby*, with passages of poetic prose when it fits the
action, but no ruminations or side-shows like *Tender*. Everything
must contribute to the dramatic movement ... Two thousand
words today and all good' (*Letters*, p. 128). Hemingway had just
published *For Whom the Bell Tolls*, and, although Fitzgerald
thought it a superficial book, he nevertheless wrote a warm letter
of congratulation to his once close friend.

Frances Kroll observed that, just when he seemed to be working at his best, he began to have recurrent dizzy spells. Late in
November, Fitzgerald had a heart attack at Schwab's drugstore
and he had to rest in bed, where he wrote for several hours each
day on a specially constructed board. Because his apartment was
on the top floor, he moved into Sheilah's ground-floor apartment,
and asked Frances to look for another suitable apartment that he
might rent. At the end of a movie premiere of *This Thing Called
Love*, which he and Sheilah attended on the evening of 20
December, he felt dizzy and had to hold on to Sheilah for support
as he walked out. The doctor was scheduled to see him the next
day. On the morning of 21 December Frances stopped by to de-
liver his mail and some typed pages, and she noticed how relaxed
he looked, although he did ask her to check his drawer to see if
some money he had placed in a book was still there, 'in case anything should happen' (Ring, *Against the Current*, p. 105). The
money was there, he told her to enjoy the weekend, and she left.

While he waited for the doctor he was eating a chocolate bar and making notes about Princeton's 1941 football team in *The Princeton Alumni Weekly*, which Frances had delivered earlier. Sheilah was listening to music Fitzgerald had recommended to her (Beethoven's *Eroica* symphony) while reading a book on music history that he had put on her reading list. He suddenly rose from his chair, grabbed the mantelpiece and fell to the floor. Sheilah tried to get help, but Fitzgerald had died instantly, at 5.15 p.m., 21 December 1940. Dorothy Parker, an old friend with

Dorothy Parker

whom Fitzgerald had reportedly had a brief affair six years earlier when both were drinking heavily, came to the Los Angeles funeral parlour where his body rested prior to being shipped to Maryland. Her husband, Alan Campbell, reported that she looked at Fitzgerald's body and quoted the remark that Owl Eyes made at Gatsby's funeral, 'The poor son-of-a-bitch.'

His funeral service, conducted by an Episcopal minister with about thirty relatives and close friends in attendance, was held in Bethesda, Maryland, and he was buried in nearby Rockville Union Cemetery. Zelda did not feel well enough to attend, and Sheilah thought it would be inappropriate for her to be there. The Catholic diocese denied permission for his burial at St Mary's Church in Rockville because he was not a practising Catholic. He was re-buried at St Mary's alongside Zelda in 1975, and before Scottie died, in 1986, she asked to be buried with her parents.

At his death, Fitzgerald had paid off most of his debts, leaving only about $12,000, most of it to Highland Hospital and to Scribners. His insurance policy covered his remaining debts and provided an annuity for Zelda and Scottie. Edmund Wilson edited *The Last Tycoon* for publication in 1941, and most of the critics were generous in their appraisal, incomplete as the novel was.

Zelda lived with her mother in the following years, returning to Highland Hospital periodically. She became increasingly religious in her last years, but she was writing another book, *Caesar's Things*, and continued to paint. In her lucid moments, she remembered Scott with deep affection and regret. In the autumn of 1947, feeling that she could no longer control her day-to-day life, she returned to Highland Hospital. In March 1948, just after midnight, a fire swept through the building and Zelda was one of nine women who died, trapped in the attic.

Thus the tragic lives of F. Scott and Zelda Fitzgerald ended.

Although Fitzgerald had said that there are no second acts in American lives, his own second act was prophesied shortly after his death by writer Stephen Vincent Benét as he appraised Fitzgerald's last novel: 'This is not a legend, this is a reputation – and, seen in perspective, it may well be one of the most secure reputations of our time' (*Critical Reputation*, p. 100). Fitzgerald would have been proud of his reputation, of his secure place in the pantheon of American writers. Like Gatsby, he remained faithful to his dream, and we, his readers, are the fortunate beneficiaries of his enduring legacy.

The gravesite, St Mary's Church

FRANCIS SCOTT KEY
FITZGERALD
SEPTEMBER 24, 1896
DECEMBER 21, 1940
HIS WIFE
ZELDA SAYRE
JULY 24, 1900
MARCH 10, 1948

"SO WE BEAT ON, BOATS AGAINST
THE CURRENT, BORNE BACK
CEASELESSLY INTO THE PAST"
— The Great Gatsby

CHRONOLOGY

1918   Completes a first draft of *The Romantic Egotist* and sends it off
        to Charles Scribner's Sons, publishers. Meets Zelda Sayre
        while stationed near Montgomery, Alabama. Scribners rejects
        his novel in August and a revised version in October. Sent to
        Camp Mills on Long Island, New York, in November, to await
        overseas duty, but the war's end prevents his departure.

1919   Discharged from the army. Now unofficially engaged to Zelda,
        Fitzgerald finds work in an advertising agency in New York City.
        In June Zelda breaks their engagement. He resigns from his
        job and leaves for St Paul, where he lives at his parents' house
        while rewriting his novel. The novel, now called *This Side of
        Paradise*, is accepted by Scribners in September, and he begins
        to find acceptance for magazine stories that were earlier rejected.

1920   Fitzgerald and Zelda become engaged again in January.
        Between January and March he publishes three short stories
        and a play in *Smart Set* and two stories in *The Saturday Evening
        Post*. On 26 March *This Side of Paradise* is published. Fitzgerald
        and Zelda are married on 3 April in New York City. *Flappers and
        Philosophers*, his first short-story collection, is published in
        September.

1921   The Fitzgeralds travel abroad in England, France and Italy from
        May to September. In August they return to St Paul where in
        October their daughter, Frances Scott (Scottie) is born.

1922   Fitzgerald's second novel, *The Beautiful and Damned*, is pub-
        lished in March and his second collection of stories, *Tales of
        the Jazz Age*, appears in September. In October the family
        moves to a rented house in Great Neck, Long Island.

1923   In April his play *The Vegetable* is published, but in November it
        fails in a try-out production in Atlantic City, New Jersey.

1924   The Fitzgeralds embark for France in April, and reside in St
        Raphael on the French Riviera. During that summer Zelda and

Edouard Jozan, a French aviator, become romantically attached. In late October the family travels to Italy, where Fitzgerald revises his new novel.

1925 On 10 April *The Great Gatsby* is published. A few weeks later the Fitzgeralds rent a Paris apartment. Fitzgerald meets Ernest Hemingway in May and Edith Wharton in July.

1926 A third collection of short stories, *All the Sad Young Men*, is published.

1927 Scott and Zelda travel to Hollywood, where he is hired to write a screenplay for a flapper film, *Lipstick*, which is never produced. He meets Lois Moran, to whom he is attracted. In March the Fitzgeralds rent a large home, Ellerslie, near Wilmington, Delaware.

1928 Return to Paris in April and to Ellerslie in September.

1929 In March the family returns to Europe, travelling to Italy and the Riviera before renting an apartment in Paris in October.

1930 Family travels to North Africa in February before returning to Paris. Fitzgerald tries to focus on his new novel, and writes a number of short stories that defray their expenses. In late April Zelda suffers her first nervous breakdown and enters the Malmaison Clinic. Several weeks later she is moved to Valmont Clinic in Switzerland and in June to another Swiss clinic, Prangins. Fitzgerald lives in Switzerland during the summer and autumn.

1931 Fitzgerald returns to the United States for his father's funeral in February. Visits Montgomery to inform Zelda's family of her condition. On his return to Europe at the end of the month, she is considerably improved and, by September, after her release from Prangins, they rent a house in Montgomery. In the autumn Fitzgerald accepts Metro-Goldwyn-Mayer's offer to go to Hollywood to work on a screenplay for Jean Harlow.

1932   Zelda's condition deteriorates at the beginning of the year and, in February, she is admitted to the Henry Phipps Clinic at Johns Hopkins University Hospital in Baltimore. Fitzgerald returns to his daughter in Montgomery. In May he rents La Paix, a house near Baltimore, where Zelda joins him in June. Her novel, *Save Me the Waltz*, which she completed while at Phipps, is published.

1933–4 After completing his novel *Tender is the Night*, Fitzgerald moves from La Paix to a town house in Baltimore in December 1933. The novel is published the following April. Zelda has another breakdown in January 1934 and is admitted to Sheppard-Pratt Hospital outside Baltimore. In March she enters Craig House in Beacon, New York, but is sent back to Sheppard-Pratt in May.

1935   Fitzgerald, ill, stays at a hotel in Tryon and then at the Grove Park Inn in Asheville, North Carolina. *Taps at Reveille*, his fourth collection of short stories, is published in March. In September he moves to an apartment in downtown Baltimore, and then to Hendersonville, North Carolina, for the winter, where he starts writing the *Crack-Up* essays.

1936   Zelda is hospitalized in Asheville in April and, in July, Fitzgerald returns to the Grove Park Inn in Asheville. His mother dies in September.

1937   Moves to the Oak Park Inn in Tryon for six months; in need of money, he accepts an offer from MGM Studios for a six-month contract in Hollywood. Meets gossip columnist Sheilah Graham in July and they begin a relationship that lasts until his death. That summer he starts the script for *Three Comrades*. The studio renews his contract in December for another year.

1938   Moves several times in California, from the Garden of Allah Hotel to Malibu to Encino, where he lives in a cottage on the estate of actor Edward Everett Horton. His MGM contract is not renewed in December.

1939   In February producer Walter Wanger hires him to work with writer Budd Schulberg on a script for a new film, *Winter Carnival*. The two go on a drinking spree to Dartmouth College, where Wanger fires Fitzgerald. He recovers in a New York City hospital, returns to California, and works as a free-lance scriptwriter. Begins work in October on a new novel about Hollywood.

1940   Zelda is released from Highland Hospital in North Carolina in April and returns to her mother's home in Montgomery. Fitzgerald dies of a heart attack on 21 December at Sheilah Graham's apartment in Hollywood – half-way through writing *The Last Tycoon* – and is buried in Rockville Union Cemetery, Maryland, on 27 December. (Re-buried at St Mary's Church, Rockville, in 1975, alongside Zelda.)

1947–8 Zelda re-enters Highland Hospital in November 1947 and dies in a fire there on 10 March 1948.

BIBLIOGRAPHY

(Works by Fitzgerald cited in the text are referred to by short title; others by author/editor surname and short title.)

Bruccoli, Matthew J., *Some Sort of Epic Grandeur* (New York: Harcourt Brace Jovanovich, 1981).

Bryer, Jackson R., ed., *The Critical Reputation of F. Scott Fitzgerald: A Bibliographical Study* (Hamden, CT: Archon, 1967).

Fitzgerald, F. Scott, *Afternoon of an Author*, ed. Arthur Mizener (New York: Scribners, 1957).

——, *All the Sad Young Men* (New York: Scribners, 1926).

——, *The Apprentice Fiction of F. Scott Fitzgerald*, ed. John Kuehl (New Brunswick, NJ: Rutgers University Press, 1965).

——, *The Beautiful and Damned*, ed. Alan Margolies (London: Oxford World Classics, 1998).

——, *Correspondence of F. Scott Fitzgerald*, ed. Matthew J. Bruccoli and Margaret M. Duggan (New York: Random House, 1980).

——, *The Crack-Up*, ed. Edmund Wilson (New York: New Directions, 1956).

——, *Flappers and Philosophers* (New York: Scribners, 1920).

——, *F. Scott Fitzgerald: A Life in Letters*, ed. Matthew J. Bruccoli (New York: Scribners, 1994).

——, *F. Scott Fitzgerald in His Own Time: A Miscellany*, ed. Matthew J.

Bruccoli and Jackson R. Bryer (New York: Scribners, 1971).

——, *F. Scott Fitzgerald's Ledger: Outline of My Life* (*A Facsimile*) (Washington, DC: NCR/Microcard, 1973).

——, *The Great Gatsby*, ed. Ruth Prigozy (London: Oxford World Classics, 1998).

——, *The Last Tycoon*, ed. Edmund Wilson (New York: Scribners, 1941).

——, *The Letters of F. Scott Fitzgerald*, ed. Andrew Turnbull (New York: Scribners, 1963).

——, *The Notebooks of F. Scott Fitzgerald*, ed. Matthew J. Bruccoli (New York and London: Harcourt Brace Jovanovich/Bruccoli Clark, 1978).

——, *The Pat Hobby Stories*, ed. Arnold Gingrich (New York: Scribners, 1962).

——, *The Price Was High: The Last Uncollected Stories of F. Scott Fitzgerald*, ed. Matthew J. Bruccoli (New York: Harcourt Brace Jovanovich/Bruccoli Clark, 1979).

——, *The Short Stories of F. Scott Fitzgerald: A New Collection*, ed. Matthew J. Bruccoli (New York: Scribners, 1989).

——, *The Stories of F. Scott Fitzgerald*, ed. Malcolm Cowley (New York: Scribners, 1951).

——, *Tales of the Jazz Age* (New York: Scribners, 1922).

——, *Taps at Reveille* (New York: Scribners, 1935).

——, *Tender is the Night* (New York: Scribners, 1934).

——, *This Side of Paradise* (New York: Scribners, 1920).

——, *Thoughtbook of Francis Scott Key Fitzgerald*, ed. John Kuehl (Princeton, NJ: Princeton University Library, 1965).

——, *The Vegetable* (New York: Scribners, 1923).

Fitzgerald, Zelda, *Save Me the Waltz* (New York: Scribners, 1932).

Hemingway, Ernest, *A Moveable Feast* (New York:Scribners, 1964).

——, *For Whom the Bell Tolls* (New York: Scribners, 1940).

——, *The Sun Also Rises* (New York: Scribners, 1926).

Ring, Frances Kroll, *Against the Current: As I Remember F. Scott Fitzgerald*

(Berkeley, CA: Creative Arts Book Co., 1985).

Tompkins, Calvin, *Living Well is the Best Revenge* (New York: Viking, 1971).

Turnbull, Andrew, *Scott Fitzgerald* (New York: Scribners, 1962).

LIST OF ILLUSTRATIONS

Every effort has been made to contact all copyright holders. The publishers will be happy to make good in future editions any errors or omissions brought to their attention.

[Note: All illustrations provided by Princeton University Library are courtesy of the Department of Rare Books & Special Collections, Manuscript Division.]